Advance Praise for

Spare Me

"Anthony is one of the funniest, smartest guys I've ever done radio with, and an unapologetically masculine man, which is an increasingly rare thing in this ever pussified world we find ourselves in."

—JOE ROGAN

ALSO BY ANTHONY CUMIA

• • • • • • • • • • • • • • • • • •

Permanently Suspended: The Rise and Fall…
and Rise Again of Radio's Most Notorious Shock Jock

SPARE ME

SPARE ME

ANTHONY CUMIA

with Johnny Russo

Post Hill
PRESS

A POST HILL PRESS BOOK
ISBN: 979-8-88845-076-5
ISBN (eBook): 979-8-88845-077-2

Spare Me

Cover design by Conroy Accord

Post Hill Press
New York • Nashville
posthillpress.com

Published in the United States of America
1 2 3 4 5 6 7 8 9 10

CONTENTS

ARTIE

● ● ● ●

THE FIRST NOTION OF POSSIBLY having a cohost for my podcast wasn't until 2017, when Keith Maresca and I went to Artie Lange's apartment in Hoboken to be guests on his own podcast.

"You know, why don't we approach Artie to be the cohost of your show?" Keith suggested. And I was thinking, "I don't know if I need one." I mean, things were going smooth at the Compound—Compound Media, the podcast platform I created—and I liked doing my solo gig, but Artie was a big name and a funny, talented guy, and I knew we would play well off each other and that he would definitely help with bringing in subscriptions to the network. So I gave Keith the okay to approach Artie with an offer.

Now, we all knew Artie had issues in the past, and he was having those same issues at the time we offered him the cohost job. This wasn't like, "Oh, remember when Artie had those problems with drugs and alcohol?" At this time, he was right in the midst of what could be argued was the worst time he'd ever had with said drugs and alcohol. So that was in my head, but I was also thinking, "Compound Media is all about the misfits of fucking radio. Let's get everybody who's fucked up and put them in one place. I don't care. How bad could it be? It'll make for great radio." So I was all for it, and so was Artie.

We offered him a hundred thousand a year, and he took it. No one else was offering Artie Lange that kind of money at that time. He was still making some scratch doing comedy gigs, but the truth is, when he would show up at a lot of these clubs, let's just say he wasn't performing as well as he could. So, we offered Artie the money, and he actually said to Keith, "I will be the exemplary employee of Compound Media." Knowing now how everything turned out, how can you not look back at that statement and laugh?

So now Artie was onboard, and his responsibility was to show up at the studio in Manhattan on Monday through Thursday from 4 p.m. to 6 p.m. That's it. It wasn't that tough a schedule. But Artie was rarely, if ever, on time, and he rarely, if ever, stayed for the whole show. There were times when Artie would go to the bathroom and never come back to the show. One of these days was his birthday. We had a big birthday show for him. We thought, "Why not have a great event for our new cohost, Artie Lange?"

We get the cake, we have a bunch of guests in the studio, the decorations are up, and Artie goes, "Yeah, I gotta go to the bathroom." He leaves, and instantly I'm thinking, "Uh-oh." Now time is ticking by, and he's not coming back. We're sitting there with a big Artie Lange cake, the candles are all lit, and he never comes back for his own birthday party that we're throwing for him.

Now, I thought this was hilarious—perfect, prime Artie Lange. He just leaves his own birthday party to go do whatever Artie does, which is probably a lot of drugs. I didn't mind his antics—I thought it was kind of cool and funny. And of course, this is why we hired Artie in the first place. It'd be outlandish to think that we hired Artie to do a real show with a real cohost who was going to be engaged in a real conversation. I mean, that wasn't even a possibility. But I saw the upside of having a guy who was so fucking unstable and out there and on drugs and just so unbelievably undependable that it was kind of funny to me. But people like Keith, who was trying to run a business, didn't find it as humorous.

I didn't care if Artie didn't show up one day. I wasn't sitting around going, "Oh my God, what am I going to do if Artie isn't here?" I did the show. That's what I do. I do solo shows, and I love it. And if Artie left early or just disappeared again, I didn't care. I can do a show by myself. So, whatever interaction I had with Artie—no matter how insane it was, no matter how undependable he was—I still thought it was funny. It was Artie being Artie: irresponsible, on drugs, fucked-up Artie Lange.

Also, aside from the fact that it was cool to have him on the show, when Artie was on his game, he was hilariously funny. He could rip people apart. He's so quick, even in an altered mental state because of drugs or what have you. You won't find someone faster or more able to burn somebody and come up with jokes about whatever topic you're talking about than Artie, even in his worst state. So, when he was there, there was no one better.

But I just knew he wasn't going to be there on any kind of predictable basis. That wasn't who Artie was. He lasted, I believe, nine months on the show. It was tough. He would show up some days completely incoherent. And even with how amazing he was with comedy and being that quick-witted, there were days when he was not even there. His body was physically in the seat, but he just was not there. And at some point, a lot of people on social media were saying, "Dude, what are you doing? You shouldn't put him out there like that, because he's fucked up." And I gave that some thought over the time that he was there. But it was who he was. I knew he wanted to be there. I knew he wanted to work. He wanted to be loyal, but his addiction just kept him from being able to fulfill any obligations he had made.

So, to get mad at him was silly. You might as well get mad at yourself if you couldn't see that. When Keith would get mad at him, I would kind of laugh and be like, "What do you expect? Have you read the story of the scorpion and the frog?" A scorpion wants to ride on a frog's back to get across a river. And the frog goes, "I'll take you across, but you have to promise not to sting me." And the scorpion goes, "Sure." And then halfway across the river, the scorpion stings him. And the frog goes, "Now we're both gonna die. Why did you sting me?" He goes, "Because I'm a scorpion."

Artie was going to be fucked up. And that's what he was on the show.

He was also constantly in trouble, whether it was legal trouble or trouble with some really nefarious people—drug dealers and bookies and whatnot. And look, I make a good living. So while it might be considered enabling, if Artie asked me for anything, I would give it to him. Not drugs, but money. Which he most likely would use to get drugs. One time he called me when I was back at my apartment after the show, and he said, "Hey, Anthony, can I swing by your place and borrow twenty-five bucks from you?" I was like, "Yeah, fuck yeah, I got that. Come on by." Ten minutes later Artie called again. "Can you make it fifty bucks?" I ended up giving him a hundred, which he repaid on air the next day.

I'm not naive. I knew what Artie needed $100 for, but I just can't refuse the guy. He's charming. People like him. You want him to like you. He's one of those people who has a great way of influencing others to do what he wants them to do for him, and I know damn well that he knows this better than anyone. You become a master of manipulation when you have an addiction like that.

There was a time he was hammered on the show, and Chris Hansen was our in-studio guest. Chris Hansen was the star of the *To Catch a Predator* TV series, where he would catch pedophiles who were after young boys and girls on the internet. I've had a professional relationship with Chris for a while; he's been on so many shows, and I find him very funny and entertaining as hell.

So Artie is sitting there next to Chris, and the entire time, Artie is asking him if he's fucking kids. Chris would be talking the way Chris does: "So we got this guy, and apparently he was trying to seduce a fourteen-year-old to have sex." And then Artie would just pop in and go, "So did you fuck her? Did you fuck that kid?" And I'm mortified, but also laughing because it's funny. I'm sitting there as the host of this show, but I'm also a fan of Artie Lange and how insane the shit he can say right to someone's face is.

So even though Chris Hansen is my guest, I'm laughing my balls off that Artie is asking a professional pedophile catcher if he's fucking children. I was so torn. As a shock jock, you go through these times when you want to put the funniest, craziest shit that you possibly can on the air. But then while you're in that host seat, you also know that these people are your guests, and they probably shouldn't be put in these uncomfortable situations. But I just couldn't bring myself to stop it. And Artie didn't stop the whole time. He just kept accusing Chris Hansen of fucking children.

You just can't bring anyone else in who's going to do that. He's going to do that because he's Artie Lange. He's got that personality—the same one, perhaps, that also drew him to doing drugs and being self-destructive. So, you take the bad with the good. The bad was sometimes Artie wasn't there, or he'd leave early or whatever. But the good was something like that, where no one else in their right mind would ask Chris Hansen if he's fucking kids.

The first time I saw firsthand that Artie dealing with issues was when Keith and I went over to his house to do his podcast. He actually ended up canceling on us. We sat down, and his producer, Dan, was there. All the equipment is set up on his kitchen table overlooking the Hudson River, across from Jersey, beautiful view, but his place looked really disheveled. Like you can tell that no one is really keeping up with it. And Artie comes in quickly and says hi. And then he leaves again. He doesn't leave the apartment; he's in there somewhere in another room, and we just don't see him again. And Dan says, "Oh, yeah, alright, he's not going to be able to do this today. We're going to have to reschedule." And I'm like, "He's right in the other room. Why doesn't he come out and say something?" Apparently, he had gotten himself pretty fucked up and wasn't able to even come in, sit down, and go through an hour of just bullshitting at his kitchen table with me.

So that was the first hint. And when we left that day, Keith and I were just kind of looking at each other with our arms up in the air going, "What the fuck just happened? What was that? He was right there." That was the first of many red flags that would pop up with Artie. He did reschedule. We did do the show, but we did notice at that point, Artie had started getting physically affected by the drugs—nosebleeds and his nose kind of collapsing, and all the stuff that drug addiction causes. Still, he was hilarious and also a very nice guy. In fact, at some point, every addict fucks up their friendships, but not Artie. He retained friendships with people he had fucked over, and it's because he's charming, nice, and funny as fuck.

So, we made him a cohost. But it wasn't very long before we realized he was still heavily using, and it was affecting his performance on the show. Sometimes he would ask us to book him a hotel room after the show was over. Six o'clock would roll around, and if he was even there until six, he'd go, "I don't want to go home. I'm just going to stay in town. Could you guys get me a hotel room?"

So, we would get him a room in a shitty hotel that was four doors down from our studio. He would go there, and we didn't know or care about what he was doing there. Four to six—that's all we gave a shit about. One time Keith went to book the room for him at the hotel, and the front desk person said, "We are not accepting any reservations for Artie Lange anymore." And Keith asked why. Apparently, the previous time Artie stayed there, he left the room looking like a murder scene. There was blood everywhere, apparently from Artie's nose. His nose was already deteriorating from drug abuse, and he had gotten punched by his dealer. He just bled everywhere on the bed. So, it was to the point where the hotel knew who he was and would no longer have him on their premises. And this wasn't the fucking Plaza or the St. Regis; this was a shithole hotel on Thirty-Fifth Street.

After nine months, having Artie on the show just got to be too much. And again, for me, I'm there four to six and just do my show, and whatever happens, I don't really care—if it's outrageous, or if it's irresponsible, or if it's childish, or if it's Artie leaving. Like I said, if it's good radio or good content, I don't give a shit. But Keith was running a business and paying this guy to be there, and a lot of times Artie would ask for advances on his pay and then not show up for the actual work part. And Keith, rightly so, was getting kind of pissed at this. So, he finally came to me and said, "You know, we might have to pull the plug and end this Artie thing." And I agreed.

It was nine months of total insanity. Anyone who has ever tried to deal rationally with an addict knows how crazy that prospect is. You just can't do it. They will not listen to reason. You can tell them something until you're blue in the face; they just won't listen. And their number-one mission is to get the next fucking high. So, to this day I still love Artie and think he's hilarious, and I root for him—as does everyone. And last I heard, he's doing very well in rehab, and I wish him all the best. But it was nine of the craziest fucking months I ever spent broadcasting. And that's really saying something.

AFTER ARTIE

● ● ● ● ● ● ●

DAVE LANDAU HAD BEEN A guest a few times during the nine-month *Artie and Anthony* experiment, and towards the end of Artie's run, Dave was sitting in as third mic and, when Artie was a no-show, as cohost. So, it made sense to offer him the chair when Artie was officially off the show for good. Dave was a popular guest on the show, and after his appearances people would point out that we had a good rapport. The truth of the matter is, I have a good rapport with anyone who comes on the show. That's a part of my fucking job.

I liked Dave and still do. As I said on Joe Rogan's podcast, Dave and I just hit it off from the start. He's got a great sense of humor, a little twisted, and a great backstory. The guy was just a fucking piece of shit for a long time. He's got so many stories about drunk driving and crashing every car he's ever had, and getting arrested fifteen times before he was eighteen. I mean, he was just a fucking disaster. But if you look at him now, he's got a great wife and a beautiful kid, he's a funny working comic, and he knows how to cohost my show. He gets it. We don't step on each other. He knows exactly what to throw in and when, so I was really happy working with Dave.

The cohost role has a couple of rules. You can't talk over the host; you have to know when to inject your own personality, jokes, and statements about the subject matter; and you have to keep things moving forward. And he was very good at that; he had a talent for being a cohost. Keith had seen all this too, and he figured that now that Artie was gone, we could take that extra money and give it to Dave.

Here's what I think Keith was thinking at the time: Artie getting a hundred grand was just Artie getting a hundred grand. He's made a lot more than that in his career. You don't know what he's going to spend it on, but you kind of know: drugs and what have you. And he's going to take it as seriously as Artie Lange, being an addict, can take a hundred grand. But Dave getting a hundred grand was a different story. This was a struggling comic. If you handed this guy a hundred grand, you'd expect to get a loyal motherfucker to come into work every day, appreciate the shit out of being on that show, and give it his best effort.

So, it was kind of a double whammy there with him. Yeah, he's good. Yes, he works well with me. But, in all honesty, we probably could have offered Dave half of that, and he would have taken it. So, we figured, alright, if we give him this much, he's going to be our guy. This money tells you we want you to be our guy. So, we gave him a hundred grand, he came on board, and it worked out well. It was a different dynamic than it had been with Artie. Anytime you get a new cohost, the whole dynamic of the show changes, whether you like it or not. And sometimes I didn't like it. In fact, I think my favorite shows are ones where I didn't have a fucking cohost. I like having a guest and talking about what I want to, but when someone is put in a position where they get the label cohost, they almost feel obligated to chime in. They are an employee now, and they feel like they have to earn their money.

Well, you really don't have to chime in on my show. You can be like a guest and sit there and say nothing. If I want to spout off for twenty minutes straight, I'll do that. It's my show. I don't think I've ever worked well with a permanent cohost since Opie, and that's only because I was the cohost in that situation. Opie was the host. I was the second guy. So that gave me much more insight into what a cohost should be. Because I was that guy for twenty fucking years. With Opie, I knew how to chime in and add what I added to the show, but not step all over shit. So, I was looking for that from anyone who would be a cohost on my own show.

Dave and I didn't have any conversations about how the dynamic would work. In fact, I've never spoken to anyone who's been on my show about how we should work together. With Dave, it was just expected that he'd know. If you're good enough that we're going to pay you $100,000 a year to sit in that second seat, you'd better know how it fucking works. I don't need to give lessons. This isn't the Connecticut School of Broadcasting. We need you to come in here and know your fucking job and do it. And if they didn't, I would get frustrated as fuck. The same thing applies to guests. I've been in situations with guests where it's like pulling fucking teeth. And it's one of the most frustrating shows you can have when you're looking at the clock thinking, "Please, please end the show already." And if your cohost is making you feel like that? Whoa, you've picked the wrong guy.

But Dave was always very good with our dynamic. We were on the same page. We went into a bit once about the shitty job of being a Long Island railroad train conductor. It's like a job from the 1800s, and they still do it the same way. They wear the dumb uniform and the dumb hat, and they have a hole puncher. It's 2024 and they're still punching holes in tickets—it's fucking *Twilight Zone* shit. And so we went off on that, going back and forth and not stepping on each other. We complemented each other, and it was perfect. That's what the dynamic with a cohost is supposed to be.

And as far as being a comic goes, I think Dave is fucking great. I've seen him live—but not until after we hired him. I had only seen him on the air with me before he came onboard. Then he had a gig at Governor's Comedy Club out on Long Island, and I went to see him, and he hit the stage, and I was just sitting there biting my lip thinking, "Please don't suck." Because if he sucked, I would lose all respect for him. I'd be like, "Oh, a hack is on my show. This is terrible." But he got up there and just destroyed it. It was amazing. And I was like, "Phew. Thank God." He was very funny, and still is. When Dave was on the show, I never had any plans of firing him or replacing him with anyone else. Him being the cohost worked out great.

Until…

Well, there is one issue that is so textbook for radio, podcasting, any kind of broadcasting, and that is that loyalty is a really difficult concept for a lot of people. Some of it I understand, and the way Dave left the show could have been handled better, to say the least, because he was on it for a few years. We went through the COVID shit together. He and I broadcasted from the home studio in my basement during COVID. Dave and one of our producers, Drew, were staying at my house. They had separate guest rooms in a separate wing of my Roslyn estate. And every day, we'd get up and do the show and have dinner together, and it was a pretty cool kind of united-front thing that we had going during this whole time. We had camaraderie, which I thought was very important. We would do special *Mystery Science Theater*–style shows in the theater with episodes of *Colombo*. We could just sit there and goof on a movie or anything else, and it would be great. I mean, these episodes of the show are still up and available online, and people love them.

So, I never thought Dave would want to leave or get an offer he couldn't refuse. Because again, aside from the rapport we had, one hundred grand isn't a bad salary for a working street comic.

But there's a show called *Louder with Crowder*, where Steven Crowder does a lot of political talk and comedy bits. It's popular; it has a following. And Steven Crowder was always asking me and Dave to come on his show and talk about things, and I know he appreciated Dave as a comic. And then I started noticing Dave doing his show a couple of times a week, and I knew how this was gonna end. I thought, "I'm not a kid anymore. I've been through this with girls, and it's a lot more devastating than with a guy comic cohost." I just knew Crowder was wooing Dave to be part of his cast on his show.

I even spoke to Dave about this. I said, "Hey, what's going on over here? Is Crowder making a move for you to be on his show?" And Dave assured me, "No." Dave then said that Crowder wanted both of us to become part of his network and his circle of influence there. Obviously, I didn't believe any of it. And then, not much later that day,

Dave sent me a resignation email. Now, this is after a couple of years of us being very tight doing a show together, him living at my house doing the show during COVID. And he sends me an *email* saying that he's going over to the *Louder with Crowder* show to be one of the few cohosts that they have over there.

Yeah, I was pissed. I felt like it was backstabbing and a little disloyal. But the thing I do understand—and this is only what I heard; I have no verification of it—is that supposedly they doubled his salary to $200,000 a year. Now, look, I'm not stupid. I have no inflated sense of self-worth. There's no way I could have paid Dave $200,000 a year. So, if it was all about money, fuck yeah, go run. And even if it wasn't all about money, that's a lot of money to turn down. So I don't fault Dave for making the best move he could possibly make for himself. Still, I felt a little betrayed.

For the most part, I don't work with contracts. I like a simple handshake. I don't want to tie anyone up, and I don't want to tie myself up, with contracts. So, when I pay someone, I tell them, "This is what you'll make here, and I don't legally hold anybody to their services." I would never say, "You can't leave. You can't do this. You're not allowed to pursue that." I never liked that approach. When I was at SiriusXM, they didn't want me to do a show from my basement during off hours. I did the *Opie & Anthony* show from 6 a.m. to 10 or 11 a.m. And they were telling me what I could and couldn't produce in my own house, that I couldn't broadcast my own *Live From the Compound* show with me drunkenly singing karaoke, because somehow it interfered with their exclusivity.

So, I've never been into that kind of thing with the people I've hired for my own show. But I also trust that the people I work with will appreciate that type of deal and know that just because something isn't in writing doesn't mean there should be no loyalty. I understand why Dave, a young guy with a wife and a kid, would decide to take double the money that I was offering. But there was that handshake and our friendship and camaraderie, and all the other stuff that went on for those years. So yeah, a bit of me was pretty pissed off about him going over there.

Doing it over email just didn't sit right with me either. Why not hang out and talk to me, let me know what's going on? Like, "This is what I'm thinking. This is what I'm going to be pursuing." You know, it's not like a boyfriend-girlfriend thing. There's not going to be tears. There's not going to be scorn or any keying of cars. It's just two guys who have worked together, with one of them going, "Hey, this is what I'm doing now." So yeah, I think the way he did it was a lot more insulting than the fact that he left for another show. It was the icing on top of the disloyalty.

But things have a way of turning out in the end. Dave is no longer with Crowder and has moved on to cohosting his own show on the Blaze network. And as for Crowder, let's just say he's dealing with his own problems at the moment.

After Dave left, I really started to doubt that there was anyone I could trust as cohost, someone who could do the job that suits my style of broadcasting, so I decided to go solo. I just didn't want to depend on anyone else anymore when it came to my show. The second you get a cohost, you have another person you have to depend on, and it's a distraction if they don't show up. "Hey, Anthony, where's Artie today?" I don't care. I'm talking about what I want to talk about. "Dude. Where's Artie? Did you hear what Dave's doing?" I'm like, no, I want to do my show. So, unless they're there every day, like you are, it becomes a distraction to what your actual show is. Which, if you ask me, is very detrimental. Then it's not an advantage any- more to have a cohost. So, I thought, "I'll do my show by myself. And I'll have guests come in at five. That gives me an hour to just vent and go over all the shit that I've looked at online and read about and watched on TV for the past twenty-four hours. I have an hour now when I don't have to worry about who's going to be sitting next to me and if they're going to be offended by what I'm saying."

Look, some guests don't like the topics of my conver- sation. But it's my fucking show. So yeah, I'm going to talk about race, religion, sexuality, all that shit, even though so many people have a problem even being in the same room as someone talking about these topics. I'd rather just blow it out myself. And then, depending on the guests, their per- sonality, what they believe in, and what they're willing to talk about, I could continue into that next hour with them doing the same shit I did the first hour, or I could completely do a U-turn and talk about what they're doing or any other topic that they're interested in and not offended by. And that's where not having a permanent cohost comes in. And that's why I like it. First and foremost, I want to do my show the way I want to do it. I'd rather just say what I want and have a guest who can chime in, who I can bounce stuff off of, every Monday through Thursday from four to six on Compound Media.

Tune in and see for yourself how much better it works this way.

KTC

● ● ●

KEITH THE COP AND I have been friends for decades now, going back to our WNEW days, when he was unbelievably constructive and productive for the *Opie & Anthony* radio show. Keith was an NYPD cop, just a uniformed officer at first, then he made it up to lieutenant, and whatever he could do to help us, he would do. One time we needed an NYPD uniform for a show where we had one of our interns dress up like an NYPD officer and then strip for somebody. And Keith showed up with a uniform, which was the first time we had ever met him. And since then, he has always helped us with everything we need. He's worked security for our shows, and me and him have become great friends. He became to me what "Club Soda" Kenny was for Opie and Dice. Keith was my guy.

He's in that friend category where you're more like brothers. That's Keith. He's a stand-up guy and one of the most loyal friends and business associates I know. He was the guy who got me off the couch when I was just sitting there drinking beers and going, "Well, I'm fired. I'm fucked. SiriusXM fired me. I'm damaged goods. That's it." And he's the one that came over and said, "Hey, you got that studio downstairs—what are you doing? Do something! Do a show!"

So, of course I'll always be grateful and indebted to him for smacking me in the head and getting me motivated to get Compound Media off the ground. He really took the reins and started making the calls that needed to be made—for internet and logistics and apps, and how much bandwidth is used, and how do you get cameras to put out HD video? And all this shit was unknown at the time, and he figured it out.

My goal was to have a show hosted by an incompetent drunk that didn't look that way. I wanted it to look professional, like the news or *The Tonight Show*. Not like a shitty webcam and a shitty PlayStation headset mic. I wanted real mics, a desk, cameras, backdrops, lighting. And then when it came to the host, people would be like, "Why does this guy have this professional setup? He's rambling and making racial jokes and sexual jokes." That was my vision for Compound Media.

Now, Keith is a little more traditional than I am when it comes to business. He wanted the business end of the show to run properly, and of course you need that. We have to pay rent in the studio. The lights have to stay on. And there's a bunch of other things that go on behind the scenes of making dick jokes for two hours, things that have to be bought and paid for. The problem was, how do we get this show out to a shitload of people for as cheap as possible? How do they subscribe? How do you build an audience? It was all this financial and logistical stuff, and that's what Keith handled. Then, once all that stuff was in place, Keith started delving into the artistic part of the network, finding shows, hiring shows, figuring out the schedule—should we have morning, afternoon, and evening shows?

I've said it many times before, and I will continue saying it in the future: I love Keith. Adore him. He was integral in getting the Compound Media model off the ground. But Keith isn't a guy who can pick on-air talent and know it's going to work. I think he made a lot of knee-jerk decisions. There were people that, my God, I wouldn't even fucking talk to today who were working for my company. So, the more the logistical end of Compound Media got taken care of and was put in place and just was on autopilot and worked, the less Keith really had to do as far as that end goes.

Still, there were constant issues with the companies that provided bandwidth and with sales and hiring that were frustrating to Keith. The shows that he would sign would be terrible. And eventually he decided he just didn't want to do it anymore. I think there was also a part of him that thought that the business stuff might eventually start affecting our friendship, and he didn't want that to happen. There were plenty of times when I would go, "What was that move?" or "Why did we do this?" or "Who is that?" But I'm so anti-confrontational that the majority of the time, even with the people I know I can approach and say, "What the fuck is this?" I won't do it. I just can't bring myself to do it, so while that might have been productive, I just never did it. I would usually just ride it out and see how it would end up and then deal with the mess after.

It wasn't like Keith was a rogue actor making every decision without my knowledge. He would always consult me on show decisions, and most of the time I would trust his judgment and say, "Alright, let's give that a try." And sometimes I would think, "Oh, yeah. That's going to suck."

In hindsight, it's probably best that Keith stepped away when he did. I don't know if our friendship would have been affected if he were still running things at Compound, and I'm glad I don't have to find out.... See you in the Palmetto State, pal.

THE MISFITS OF
COMPOUND
● ● ● ● ● ● ● ● ●

AS I MENTIONED IN THE last chapter, instead of just me doing a show for Compound Media, Keith thought we needed other shows, which was an idea I liked. In fact, I had delusions of grandeur, of being the king of a broadcasting empire. So, we brought other shows onboard for mornings, afternoons, and evenings. Some of them have been successful and some haven't. Some I've really enjoyed, and some not so much.

Now, the business model of a lot of podcasts associated with podcasting networks is that the networks don't actually pay for the shows. The shows have to get their own advertising. The network is basically doing the podcasters a favor by putting them on and giving them the equipment and the connection to the internet. And the podcasters' job is to make money through advertising. Nowadays, Patreon and YouTube are additional money-making avenues. For all of these avenues, most networks take half the income.

When we started the Compound Media Network, however, we would bring these new shows on and actually pay the talent. One of the shows we brought onboard was *In Hot Water*, with comedians Geno Bisconte and Aaron Berg. I wanted comics on the shows. I don't like shows that just have some dude who thinks he can sit there and pontificate for an hour and it's going to be entertaining. Comics are supposed to be funny at least. They're degenerates. They're dirty. They have something to say. It's interesting. So, I wanted the majority of the shows that we were going to bring on to be helmed by comedians.

For Geno and Aaron's podcast, it was another situation where we didn't have contracts. As with everyone else, I just thought about loyalty and hoped that they would abide by the rules of being honest dudes.

Now, I make it a habit of not poking my fucking nose into other shows on my own network. I don't care what they talk about; I don't care what language they use. Our platform is subscription-based. So, I don't have to worry that someone's going to inadvertently tune in and hear something that offends them. If you hear it, someone is paying for it in your house. So, take it up with them. Don't take it up with me. Now, you have someone like Geno who is a volatile and bombastic guy, but I love him. He's funny. He's a pisser to hang out with, and he drinks like me. But he's been known to use language that could be a bit offensive to other people, especially his Jewish cohost.

So, after a couple of years of doing the show, Aaron had probably built up some passive-aggression toward Geno. And it became more and more apparent that he wasn't very happy with Mister Bisconte's antics. And look, I don't even totally blame him. There were gigs I was at where Geno was completely incoherent onstage. And Aaron had put these gigs together, and so he had to talk to the club owner as to why one of the comics was literally stumbling off the stage. I get it. I understand his frustration. But again, he signed on to work with Geno. He knew the guy he'd be working with.

Eventually, the Gas Digital Network, which is run by the *Legion of Skanks* comics, recruited Aaron to go over there. So, he left Compound Media. And he alluded to how he didn't like the political incorrectness at Compound Media. Occasionally someone on a show will drop the N-bomb, or make some very inappropriate sexual or racial jokes. And I know Aaron loves these jokes. But when you're trying to reach a wider audience, you have to turn your back on some things that you absolutely enjoy and find funny.

That's what's happening these days with a lot of comics. And I think it's dishonest. And I think they're only lying to themselves. Because I've seen Aaron's show plenty of times, and it's very funny, but it would be insane to say it's politically correct or family friendly. He's saying shit that is unbelievably offensive. So, trying to claim that he's not at Compound Media anymore because we're this horribly offensive platform is kind of hypocritical.

But, hey, I wish Aaron the best. And as for Geno, he still has a show on Compound Media. At least at the time of this writing he does.

You never know with Geno. He's at the center of all the drama. Next came an incident where Pat Dixon got to live out the dream of many who have met Bisconte: he broke Geno's jaw.

File this one under, "One of those things that I never wanted to deal with."

I don't like being the boss of a company. I love doing my show, and I love having Compound Media, but I don't love running it because I'm not that guy. And I have to be every so often. So, when things pop up that need the attention of the boss, I do have to step up. And this was one of those occasions when that was necessary.

A little backstory: Compound Media has so many conflicting personalities in its work environment. There are people who hate each other, and some who want to kill each other, and then there's the underlying fact that a lot of comics are narcissistic psychopaths. I mentioned earlier about wanting to have only comics do shows, but for most comics, it comes with a caveat. Comics are all insane. Every single one of them has mental fucking problems, and they don't know how to deal with people. They don't know how to live in a civil society. They're just full of resentment, hate, self-hatred, daddy issues, whatever it is. They find it hard to communicate with each other.

At the time of the incident, Geno was the host of *In Hot Water*, and Pat Dixon was hosting *Crime Report*, both on Compound Media. So, on one hand we've got Geno, who in and of himself is a nutjob, and who thoroughly likes his whiskey, which is a bad combination. He's also a button-pusher. The guy loves fucking with people. And while sometimes he says he never meant to fuck with someone, I think deep down he knows what pisses other people off, and that's exactly what he does.

On the other hand, we have Pat Dixon—who, while being a very funny guy, is a little strange, to say the least. And Pat had just broken up with a girl, and Geno in his infinite wisdom of how to fuck with people's minds, decided to put this girl on his show. Pat texted Geno, saying in no uncertain terms, "Don't put the girl on the show." And what does Geno do? He puts the girl on the show, because Geno will just press buttons.

From what I heard, Pat texted Geno again after the show and wrote something to the effect of, "If you don't come to the bar across the street from the studio, apologize, or at least explain yourself, I'm going to punch you." Well, Geno didn't see the text before he got to the bar. And Pat, being a man of his word, walked in and punched Geno in the face.

I didn't actually see it happen, but I was sitting maybe ten feet away in my usual seat, doing my show prep. So now I had to deal with my midday guy getting belted by my evening guy. And this was no love tap. Pat broke Geno's jaw.

Luckily, it was all caught on the bar's security cameras, and we got to watch the footage over and over again to endless hilarity. I mean, holy shit, I'd never seen anyone hit someone else that hard before. Pat got Geno good. He didn't hold back at all.

Now I'm put in an uncomfortable fucking position. Look, when one employee belts another employee in the face, the boss is obligated to fire the guy. And like I said, I hate this. I'm not that guy. I don't like having to do boss shit. And, truth be told, I wasn't going to fire Pat until I knew how serious the damage was. When I found out that Geno literally had a broken jaw and had to go to the hospital, and they had to put a fucking plate in, I was like, "Shit, I guess now I gotta do something." First of all, just because, as a guy, you gotta step up and do something. Second, any lawyer would tell you that if you don't fire him and the guy hurts someone else in the future, you're liable to get sued because you didn't do anything. So, I did something. I fired Pat.

Didn't want to do it, but as they say in the old country, "My hand was forced."

Luckily, Pat got another gig hosting *The New York City Crime Report* on my old buddy Gavin McInnes' streaming platform, Censored.TV.

Gavin is like me. He's a satirist. He does parody. I consider him one of the most brilliant satirists out there. His only crime has ever been that he's too good at it, so some people don't know he's making jokes. They take it seriously and believe that he's some insane right-wing maniac—the leader responsible for the violent vigilante group known as the Proud Boys, which is a media narrative that's a whole load of bullshit.

Gavin was a leader of a group of fans of his that he decided should get together every so often; they'd have some beers in a bar and talk about how awesome America is. And that was turned into this insane right-wing nonsense that people believe Gavin started, which just isn't true.

Gavin's amazing. He's such a funny guy. He's irreverent. He's a provocateur. He likes doing things that get people mad, but he's always doing it based on humor. He does have his controversial beliefs; it's not like he's lying. Like, he believes women are best suited to be moms and wives, and should not enter the business world and give up their opportunities to become mothers and wives. And I don't know, maybe when you look at the way things have ended up, the guy might have a valid point. So, he's always on the cutting edge of what people are talking about and what's controversial, and we at Compound Media obviously thought that would make a great show, and it did.

But again, I don't hold people to contracts. And while Gavin was doing his show with us, the Blaze network offered him a shitload of money to go over there. As I said, I'm not going to be the guy who holds someone back from pursuing their best interest, but now I had to deal with losing a personality from my slew of shows. Still, I think it's way better to deal with that than to have someone resent the shit out of you for holding them to a contract and not allowing them to take a good opportunity.

So, Gavin went off and worked for Blaze for a little while. After that ended—and I don't know how, when, why, or who was responsible for that—me and Gavin decided to do a show every Wednesday together, and it's now one of the highest-rated shows on both of our platforms. People love it. We get along great. There's a dark sense of humor there, which I love. And we have the ability to talk about anything, completely uncensored.

And that's the only way you're ever going to get anything out of myself or Gavin. If we're restrained by anything, I don't really want to talk about it. I love the format that we both have. We can just spout off about all the taboos—the race stuff, the sex stuff, the transgender stuff—openly and honestly without anyone fucking with us.

I love doing our show every Wednesday, on Compound and Censored, at 4 p.m. Tune in, won't you?

As happy as I was that Gavin came back to Compound, I was equally happy to see someone leave. Which brings us to Kevin Brennan.

I think Kevin Brennan, as a comic, is very funny. I find him very entertaining. But everyone has a problem with this guy. I don't think there's one person in the industry who hasn't at some time or another had an issue with Kevin. He's obnoxious; he's unreasonable. But again, I'm running a sanctuary for misfit toys. My Compound Media is where you can go when no one else will have you. That's kind of how the whole thing got started. And Kevin fit in that scheme perfectly, because no one wants this guy. He could obviously get stage time—he's funny as a stand-up—but club owners and other acts have had major problems with him.

So, yeah, a normal person wouldn't want to bring him onboard. But since all I give a shit about is what's funny, I want that on the platform, even if it's outrageous or causes trouble. So, we gave Kevin Brennan a show on the network called *Burning Bridges*. It was called that because obviously that's what he does. And it was going great at first.

But then he had to start shitting on us—Compound Media and me and Keith the Cop and every other show on the platform. And I don't tell people what they can or can't put on their show. I'll let them do the show they want to do. But I will have opinions on it. And my opinion on this is, why would Kevin decide to just shit all over everybody involved with my company, when we're employing him?

I don't think Kevin ever gets fired. I think he leaves right before people can fire him, because he knows it's coming. He can feel it. So, he left Compound Media when he was doing *Burning Bridges*. And everybody was fine with it: "Whatever you want to do, Kevin, feel free."

Then he showed up at the studio one day out of the blue and said, "Oh, I was around the neighborhood, and I followed the FedEx guy in and got through the locked door." And I'm just thinking, "Alright, come on, sit down. Let's have some fun and talk and do a show."

Because again, I don't hold grudges. I know he's very toxic and very abrasive. But as long as we know that, why not have him on? It makes for entertaining broadcasts. So, he comes on for a show and we have a good time. And I tell him after, "What are you doing on Thursdays? Why not just come in every other Thursday? I'll pay you." And he goes, "Okay." So he starts coming on the show, and it's good. People like it. He's funny.

Then it turns into a once-a-week gig. I pay him probably one hundred dollars for a two-hour show. It's all we want from him, two hours for a hundred bucks, which he can use for gas or whatever. And that works for a little while, but like with any other thing in his life, Kevin's got to fuck it up. He's got to be self-destructive. And again, he just starts shitting on everything and everyone, which eventually leads to a big altercation with—who else?—our very own Geno Bisconte. Because, as we all know, Geno can push his buttons, and Kevin loses his temper and starts chasing Geno around the studio.

Geno has to lock himself in the engineering booth while Bob Levy holds Kevin back to try to keep him from being charged with murder. I absolutely think Kevin would have killed Geno at that moment. He was so mad at him. There's a famous video clip that came out of it, where Kevin is yelling to Geno something to the effect of, "You fucking faggot, I'll kill you! You fucking faggot!" You can see the genuine anger in Kevin's face.

At this point, I'm really concerned that someone's about to be murdered in my studio. But it just goes hand in hand with the theory that comics are nuts. And if you choose to depend on comedians for your business, *you* should be a mental patient. Ask any comedy club owner this, and they will tell you the same fucking thing. Same goes for podcasting. Comics are insane people who have figured out a way to keep themselves out of a mental institution or jail or something even worse. This little thing called stand-up keeps them out. But it doesn't make them any less nuts, or any less undependable, or any less fucking psychopathic than any other mental patient out there wandering the streets at any given moment.

In conclusion, I'm now out of the Kevin Brennan business. As everyone else should be too.

OPIE, WHAT ARE YOU DOING?

● ● ● ● ● ● ● ● ●

THE OPSTER. GREGG HUGHES. WHAT is this guy doing? Seems to me all he does is go on Facebook Live, which I think is his new "platform." And he gets maybe one hundred views (I think I could be overselling that number), and he calls out the people in the chat room: "Hey, Mike, how are you doing?" "Beverly is here." "Thanks, Pam, for hanging out." He does this while people are starting to tune in.

Now, I do a lot of what they call streaming. I'll be playing some Call of Duty and talking about random shit. But I don't get on and then wait for people to enter the chat room. So what if you miss the first few things I say? You have to get right into the conversation. But he'll sit there and just wait for people to get into the room. (John

Melendez, a.k.a. "Stuttering John," does this too.) If you have so few people you know are reliably going to come into the chat room every show, and you have to wait until they get in there and call them out, then you're in a very sad situation. Opie does this all the time.

What he does is not a show. And I've talked about this on my show *Who Are These Podcasts?* And on other Compound shows. Opie refuses to do a show, because he lacks confidence and doesn't want people to go, "Oh, but compared to Joe Rogan, your show sucks." This way he can just say, "Doesn't matter; it's my own thing. It's not a show. I'm just talking and chilling, rapping with the people, man."

Opie is petrified of criticism. He's petrified of failing again, so he doesn't want to put something out there that people would consider an entertainment program and then have to be judged against other ones. So, he goes on his whatever-it-is and calls out other legitimate programs that have guests and topics and actual listeners, and says how much better his is. Except he does nothing but take listener questions and then get annoyed because the questions are all about me, the old *O&A* show, Jimmy Norton, Sam Roberts, or Erik "Erock" Nagel. He'll feign disgust in his baby voice: "Ah, again? Really? Really? We're going to talk about this again?"

Doesn't this dummy know that it's solely up to him whether or not to take a question? Hey, Opie, maybe have a list of topics to pivot to if you get questions that you don't want to answer. Have a conversation with the viewers about something you're interested in. But he won't do that, because that would entail having an interest in anything.

The man is completely devoid of passion—about *anything*. In my opinion, it's almost sociopathic. I have never discussed anything with him that he seemed genuinely excited to talk about. I can sit there and talk about certain topics of the day that I'm not necessarily super interested in, but I make the best of it. Then there are topics I am very passionate about and enjoy talking about. And I enjoy enlightening people on those topics.

I swear to Christ, in all the years I've known Opie, I've never seen this fucker excited to discuss anything. Everything he does is based on how people will perceive him. So, he's never really passionate about anything. He just wants to put something out there, like, "Oh, I went on vacation. I went to Turks and Caicos, played golf. It was great, man." But even when he talks about his vacation, it's just not passionate. Because more than enjoying his vacation himself and wanting to convey how awesome it was to loved ones or family or fans, he just wants to boost his image so other people can be like, "Wow. God, it must be so great to be him." That's been Opie forever.

There's another part of him that will absolutely convince himself that things happened in a way they didn't. Aside from Opie, I've never seen this in real life—only in movies about sociopaths, serial killers, things like that. But I've never seen another real person I've been involved with who can witness a situation and convey the story of it a few years later with a completely different description. He has no basis in reality anymore. And it's not even like he's lying. He believes it. That is his new interpretation of what happened.

So, when he says stuff about me like, "Patrice O'Neal said Anthony is a racist and a terrible guy," Opie actually believes that, and there's no convincing him any different. It's almost like he might be mentally ill. It's different than with Stuttering John. Stuttering John is stupid. Opie is also stupid, but he might also be mentally ill too. In my opinion, of course.

The day after I did *The Howard Stern Show* where I was doing a contest with Jackie Martling, Opie was convinced I was leaving to join Howard. Like a little bitch, he said, "Oh, Howard's calling you, man. Howard's calling you and that's it. You're going over there." He was convinced of it, and I couldn't tell him anything to the opposite effect. I'm like, "Opie, I'm not going anywhere. We have our own thing going." He said, "Oh no, Howard will call you tomorrow. You were too good. Did he call you? He called you, right?"

I actually believe in Opie's head, he believes Howard called me. And to this day, he probably would say, "So, Howard called Anthony and said he wanted him for the show. But then Anthony came up and did my show instead." He's done this for years. He just comes up with these make-believe scenarios.

He can't be happy with just getting maybe a few hundred views on his videos. The ones where he just talks about his doggy: "Hey, doggy. Look everyone, it's my doggy. Whoa, look at that, it's a seagull. A seagull just flew over the beach. Isn't that insane?"

So, whenever he's doing anything that does not entail myself or Jimmy or Sam, no one watches. And he's aware of this, and the one thing Opie knows from being on the radio since he was eighteen years old is that you go with what works. So, if talking about us is what gets him the views and the clicks, he's going to keep talking about us regardless of whether it's good, bad, or neutral. Doesn't matter if it's lies or real shit that happened.

Believe me, there's plenty of real shit that occurred—if he wanted to do these *O&A* retrospectives without bashing me, he could do that. There's plenty of material that's not about just bashing me and Jimmy and Sam or anyone else. But he knows the bashing videos are the ones that get hits.

On one of his live streams, he said, "The *O&A* show ran its course." No, it didn't. We could still be doing a version of the *O&A* show. Now, would we be throwing shit on girls in fifty-five-gallon drums? No, of course not; the environment has changed. But is there a way to discuss controversial topics and have funny guests on, and be able to sit there and look at each other's miserable faces for four hours? Fuck yeah.

The show did not run its course. Opie ran its course. He was the one who was all fucking pissy about what the show was developing into, because it became more about Anthony and Jimmy than about Opie and Anthony.

I've mentioned this before, and I fully believe it: Opie's in-laws hated the show and the jokes we made about race, sexuality, politics, the poor misfortune of others, etc. They hated it, and he probably had to hear it from them all the time. And he was probably like, "I want to change this. We're going to do a cooking show with Carl Ruiz." Or whatever he imagined would be post–Opie and Anthony and Jimmy. It failed.

And he just wants to make it seem like my racist ranting brought the show to an end. Everyone knows I was saying racially based shit on the show long before I got fired in 2014. My persona on the air, although it's based on who I am, was very harsh, very outspoken, and we were able to work with it. It wasn't like a Fox News broadcast. Dru Boogie would cut songs out of my racist rants. Jimmy would start laughing and calling me a mental patient, and it was hilarious.

The years when Barack Obama was president were hilarious, and a lot of people felt the way I did. And Opie just sees what I said as racist ranting. Yeah, I was assaulted in Times Square by a black woman, and I voiced my opinion about it.

It's typical Opie. Typical phony liberal attitude, just like Stuttering John has. What was I doing? Just walking around in Times Square snapping pictures. And some black woman smacked me because she felt entitled. And I'm a racist because I talked about it. Get the fuck out of here.

I take responsibility for what I said, but I don't apologize for it. It was a hell of a rant, but there were no slurs thrown in there. I said that the behavior was savage, and that there was a problem with violence in the black community. It was, and there is.

Racist rant? Fuck you. It was an accurate rant. Sorry, Opie, if the company you worked for (that failed miserably after I was gone) couldn't deal with the truth. That it had to kowtow to the likes of Reverend Al Sharpton and every other douchebag that sees the same problem I did but didn't want to fucking acknowledge it, and instead used me as a scapegoat.

"Oh, what a racist!" Why? For saying the black community is violent? For saying that something has to be done? I'm a racist? Blow me! Hey, Opie, who do you think stole the mirrors off your car, dummy? (The mirrors got stolen off his SUV when he parked on the street because he didn't want to pay for indoor parking.) Who do you think did that? Me? Someone who thinks like me? Someone who spouts racist diatribes like me? No, it was most likely one of the people I was fucking talking about, you dumb shit.

Opie turned into another one of these liberal dopes. Stuttering John went hardcore liberal to try to win back the love of his transgender son/daughter. But he's not really liberal. He said horrible racist things over the course of years before that. He went liberal for a reason. He's most likely trying to regain the admiration of a girl who he fucked over so badly that she decided to cut her tits off and become a boy.... If he thought I was wrong, John would have probably threatened to sue me. (He did.) That litigious schmuck. C-C-Cease and desist.

Opie, on the other hand, went hardcore liberal because he thought it would get him a job at some point. The guy is sixty years old for fuck's sake. What are you doing? No one's going to be knocking on your door because you're anti-racist or pro–Joe Biden or you got vaxxed. Go over to WCBS-FM and spin some oldies. I would actually feel good for the guy if he went over to Scott Shannon and said, "Scott, so how're you doing? Mind if I get a shift? I could spin some oldies." But no. He'll talk out of his ass like he's a liberal, just hoping that the call comes in from a big station to put a young, vivacious Opie on the airwaves again—to be that rebellious young American. Not gonna happen.

But yeah, it was all my fault? It was my racist diatribe that caused the show to end? My racist persona during all the years that we were on *O&A* was an attraction. A ton

of people tuned in and enjoyed the offshoots of those diatribes—the Dru Boogie songs and the countless bits based
on them that our production staff would put together. To
say nothing of the phone calls we'd get from listeners—
both the ones who were pissed and the ones who agreed.

You think they were calling because you were playing
Candy Crush, Opie? "Hey, dude. Oh, how's the Candy
Crush going?"

Believe it or not, Jimmy and I were the rational people
in that situation. I knew what was going on. Opie would
complain that the audience share was dropping. Well,
yeah, we were shock jocks in our fifties. How about a dose
of reality, Opie? Why the hell do you think I wanted to
sign five-year contracts? Whenever our contract negotia-
tions would come up, I always wanted to sign a five-year
deal. But not Opie: "No, a one-year deal is all I want to
sign!" Because again, he thought some company was going
to magically call up and go, "You two kids are going to be
stars of my network!" Take the five-year deal, dummy. But
he had this overblown sense of self-worth, thinking that he
and Carl Ruiz were going to make something huge, perhaps bigger than O&A in its heyday was? No.

While Carl is a funny guy, Opie is comedy kryptonite
to anyone who's with him. By the way, anyone is twice as
funny without Opie as they are with him. So, if someone's
funny with Opie, they're hilarious without him. That's just
how it is.

Management knew it too. After I was fired and Jimmy left the show, management was looking for places to shove Opie. Put him behind the refrigerator or under a carpet somewhere. They didn't like him personally, and they certainly didn't like him professionally. They heard all the griping, like, "This guy's not good. He stinks. He's terrible by himself." And shit worked out the way it did.

Clearly, Jim and Sam having a show at Sirius still bothers Opie to this day. He's constantly shitting on them and saying that if he had a "show," he could easily beat them in the ratings. Can you believe that?

Again, there's Stuttering John, who is a clown. And then there's Opie, who's also a clown, but on another level. They're two different things. While John would say stuff like that, he'd never believe it. He cannot possibly have the confidence to believe that he's better than anybody. Stuttering John, in my opinion, is just a terrible person (which maybe drives him to try to steal money).

But Opie believes it, and that's sick. Opie believes he can run circles around Jimmy and Sam with what he's doing now. Now, regardless of how you feel about Jimmy and Sam, they're doing a fucking show. They're getting great guests. They've re-upped their contract. And, as with any other show, some people like it and some people can't stand it. But for Opie to actually believe that he runs circles around Jimmy and Sam with what he does with his phone at his house is absurd.

The one question I have for Opie is, "What are you doing?" And that's something I've never gotten an answer to. All I ever see is him talking shit about other people, and when he's not shit-talking, what is he talking about? Has he ever covered a topic? One fucking topic about something that he might have to form an opinion on? It goes back to the fact that he's a passionless guy who doesn't have an opinion on anything.

He'll write stuff on Twitter (X) like, "Hey, Biden's speech was awesome," or, "Hey, Fauci, good job." Is he trolling? Why wouldn't he say why he thinks they're doing a good job? Again, in my opinion, he's mentally ill, but he's also stupid. And I think the stupidity is the main reason he just doesn't have anything to say. Throw a topic out there and talk intelligently about it, Opie. But no, he's just incapable.

So again, I ask you, Opie. What are you doing?

THE STUTTERING
BUFFOON
● ● ● ● ● ● ● ● ●

LET ME START BY SAYING how utterly useless I think Stuttering John is as an entertainer, as a father, and over-all, as a human being. The only time he is entertaining at all is when clips of his show are played on *Who Are These Podcasts?* or *The Uncle Rico Show* to point out how incredi-bly stupid he is. How incredibly untalented, unfunny, hyp-ocritical, nasty, belligerent, and jealous he is, and how he projects everything that he is onto other people. He's big on projection. He's just terrible in every way.

There is not an ounce of entertainment on his show unless it's being dissected and ridiculed by other podcasts. He loves to say what an amazing personality and legend he is, although he's got to bring up shit from thirty years ago, and sometimes even longer ago, to do it. I remember a show where he was telling his fans how his elementary school drama teacher had praised him for a part he did in an elementary school play. Can you fucking imagine having to delve back into your elementary school drama production to say, "My teacher told me I was like Shake-Shakes-Shakespeare," or "My teacher thought I was like Laurence Olivier, Laurence Olivier, Lawrence's liver?"

I guess he has to go back that far because everything he's doing now is just abominable. And the worst part is, it's just boring. So, every so often, he's got to go off and make some drama about some of the people in the business, and of course I fall into that category.

Similar to Opie, he knows that talking about me and Jimmy is his only way of getting more than three hundred people to watch one of his videos. He can barely break three hundred views if he's not talking about me, Jimmy, Sam, or the *O&A* show, but he does it because he knows he's going to get more heat. So, he can't stop.

So, people like Opie and John, they all fall into one category. Which is robbing their listeners of money in exchange for utter and complete garbage. Also, what Stuttering John does these days—and he's getting to be a professional at it—is make legal threats. He's threatened me with legal action, and I find it hilarious. He told me, "I was on the phone with my lawyer today, and a lawsuit is coming down the pike."

If there's one person I feel sorrier for than John's ex-wife and kids, it is John's lawyer. If he even has one; I don't even know. I just know from what I've seen over the years that John lies about everything. He lies about his career. He lies about money. He lies about friends and business and coworkers in the entertainment business.

How do you know if he's ever telling the truth about anything? He has often on his own show spouted this nonsense about lawsuits, like, "I sued Sharon Stone, Sharon Stone, Sharon Rock." So, I went on my show and on social media a few months ago, and I said something to the effect of, "John wants to sue me and is threatening to sue me." He said in response, "You talk to my lawyer, you criminal!" He doesn't want to mention me by name. So, he calls me "criminal" and "pockface," and says I'm a pedophile and whatever other nonsense he can come up with.

And by the way, I have discussed all of these false accusations at length on my show. Have I gone out with younger girls? Sure. Were they all over the age of consent? Of course, they were—every single one of them. So, John, how about looking up the definition of the word "pedophile." It's not someone who goes out with women who are of legal consenting age to have sexual intercourse. Sorry. But you should have known that, being that you're supposedly a renowned member of Mensa. Which is another lie. John has never been in "Mensa, Mesa, mesopause." And by the way, the day will never come when I start asking myself, "What would Stuttering John think about who I'm dating?" Who the fuck is this guy? This is a guy who goes to Pickwick's Pub in the bowels of Los Angeles and picks up grandmothers. So, what do you want to do, John? Do you want to fuck a grandma or a twenty-six-year-old? You know, I'd probably opt for the twenty-six-year-old, even if I have to eventually bite her on occasion.

As for "pockface," yes, I've talked about my horrid childhood when I was dealing with cystic acne. I was getting giant fucking wounds on my face, and I had to actually cultivate a personality around it. It was terrible. They didn't really have the right medication for it until I was in my thirties, when I started taking Accutane. And then my acne actually cleared up, but you know, the damage was already done. We all have our crosses to bear and our scars and whatnot. And that's part of who I am.

As for the "criminal" part, I've talked about it ad nauseum. The Anthony Cumia–Dani Brand domestic dispute that went on at the house, where I was arrested. And then the rehab and the fucking court, and I talked about it all on social media and on my show many times. There is nothing that John is saying that's a "gotcha" moment. There's no, "My God! Look at this! Look at what he did!" Don't forget it's all in a book. I literally wrote a book about it. So, he should know he's not going to get anywhere with those arguments. And as far as having a criminal record? Nope, it doesn't exist.

I've talked about that too. Yes, when you get arrested, you go up on criminal charges. And then your job as a citizen is to utilize all the laws and not be a criminal anymore. That's how it works. So, my case was brought down to a violation. Not even a misdemeanor. It's the same level as a ticket. And it was expunged. I don't have a criminal record. I'm not a criminal, John.

I don't think you'll find another person who has talked more about those things than me, myself, and I. I discuss everything on the show and on streams, and on other shows, and in my books. John, there are no secrets. You're not going to come up with an ace card up your sleeve that's going to foil me.

I don't care if John says I'm a criminal. I just find it interesting that he has to bring these things up when I'm saying that, in my opinion, he's grifting money from people. Every indication I've seen is that Stuttering John has taken money from people for a cancer cause that is an apparition. It's just fucking a ghostly thing. The money went into his own personal account, which he then was going to divvy up? How would you know what funds are for what?

Here's what he's actually telling people: "There is a beloved chatter whose beloved one... the beloved chatter's loved one is getting chemo. They want to remain anonymous—a total anonymous entity. So, I will not bring up their name, but I will send the money, but send it to my personal account." Hilarious.

Now, *Who Are These Podcasts?* did a brilliant breakdown over hours of this whole thing. So, if you want to really catch up on the details of it, go look up the show. But any idiot could just look and see that you can't do what John is doing. That it's illegal. That it's against the terms of service for whatever platform he's using to get funds. I can't just go on my show and say, "Oh my God, some kid I know has leukemia, and it's terrible. Childhood leukemia. Isn't that bad? Can you subscribe to Compound Media? And I'll make sure I give some of that money to childhood leukemia research. Don't worry, I'll do it. Hey, I'm just trying to be a nice guy." You're not allowed to do that, you big dope.

But he goes on his show, talking about how I'm a criminal and how I'm accusing him of starting a fake cancer scam, and I'm not even being subtle here. Yes, based on everything I know about Stuttering John personally, having known him for years, having seen the way he acts with people, having heard what he's said to people—the blatant lies that I've seen him tell—I will absolutely say that I believe he has been stealing money under the guise of curing cancer.

There now, go get your lawyer, John. Get your lawyer for another non-lawsuit. Sue me. I won't show up in court. I won't answer the summons. I won't pay you. I won't do anything. I'll move to South Carolina, and you can try to chase me down there. Whatever you want to do, you blithering fool, go ahead. Your lawyer must be a real dope. Do you have pictures of him blowing men? Why would he even take your call? I wouldn't take your call whether I was a lawyer, a baker, or a goddamn candlestick maker. Tinker Tailor Soldier Spy. It's John. Fuck this idiot. If I were his lawyer, I wouldn't be picking up the phone. I don't know how you got this guy on the phone. Again, I think that's a lie too.

John, you're an idiot. I genuinely think you can be classified a borderline retard. You are a drooling, inept, low-IQ piece of shit and a fucking horrible father.

Yeah, sue me, John. I swear, please. I embrace the idea of someone coming to my studio and serving me with papers from the likes of Stuttering John Melendez. Where's my c-c-cease and desist? C-c-cease and knock it off?

So, he's been talking in his chat room about how a loved one needs chemo, and it's hilarious. John supposedly told the person he would do something, and they went, "Hey, please keep it on the QT. I don't want people to know who we are." And John goes, "Sure I'll do that." So he tells people to send money to his account. Then he gets upset if anyone believes that he might be misappropriating some of these funds. But he can't figure out why. It's because you're an asshole, John. You've been an asshole your whole life.

And, of course, you'd do anything to get more money. You blew through every penny you made. You didn't make much on *Howard Stern*. We know you were making somewhere in the realm of $30,000 to $35,000 a year there. You stayed there forever. You finally left, but you stayed there before that making shit money for what? The fame? Was that more important than money? The ability to go out and hear someone yell, "Hey, that's Stuttering John!" And you can go, "Yeah, yeah, that's me." That kind of fame was more important? It was more important than being there for your fucking family, John? $35,000 a year.

John, maybe you should have moved on and done something different, like getting another job. But, no, you're the world-famous Stuttering John Melendez. What a joke. So, you lost your fucking family. And then Jay Leno decided to fuck with Howard Stern by stealing one of his guys. That's really what it was. If you thought for two seconds that Jay fucking Leno looked at Stuttering John and said, "Goddamn, I need this guy on my show. *The Tonight Show* can't succeed without Stuttering John as the announcer," you're an idiot. It was a goof for two minutes.

And the person who realized it first was fucking Jay Leno. And then all the other people who work over there realized it too. Jay was probably thinking, "Now what do we do? We got saddled with this fucking idiot." There are plenty of interviews where Jay says that having a conversation on *The Tonight Show* with John was very awkward. There was just no chemistry there. It was terrible. So, a lot of times he'd throw it to Kevin Eubanks, the leader of the show's band, and they'd bounce off each other, and there was really nothing left for John to do.

So, they made John a writer. He loves plugging that too: "I was the announcer and then a writer for *The Tonight Show*." You were the announcer as a joke, John. Howard had a beef with Jay, and Jay figured the best way to jab Stern was to cough up some of that corporate NBC money and steal John away. And then they realized what a mistake they'd made. John was so fucking bad at the announcing job, and at doing street interviews without Howard and the show's writers coming up with shit for him to say. *The Tonight Show*'s producers were like, "What do we do with this guy?" So, they threw him in as a writer. He sat in a room with a bunch of other people to write shit for *The Tonight Show*. And they would just, you know, ignore him. They weren't going to take any of his bits.

"Yeah. Okay, John. Yeah, great bit, great bit," then they'd ignore him and do other things. I heard when Jay found out that John hadn't written any of the questions he spouted off on Howard's show, he was pissed, but I think he actually knew that before he hired John. John had to know that it was purely a move to stick it to Howard, and they were just using John as the fucking buffoon that he is: "Put him on camera. He's goofy. People know him from *Howard*. Fuck it."

And then in a short time, they were like, "Oh, this guy is terrible. Get him off camera. Put him behind the scenes." So, the first opportunity they had to get rid of him, they did. But he uses "from *The Tonight Show*" like a plug. Oh,

Jesus Christ. Really? You want to use that as a plug? You were there as a joke. You *are* a joke.

So, back to John's fake-cancer scam. He hilariously stated on his show that anyone who knows him would know that his OCD would prevent him from ever stealing or lying. Again, I saw this on *Who Are These Podcasts?*, and I can't stress enough how great a job they did with this John material. And I was sitting there listening to this and screaming. That's when I decided I needed to talk about this. I wanted to be involved so badly.

Understand what he actually just said: his OCD makes it impossible for him to commit a crime or lie. Can you even comprehend this? He's like the robot Bishop in the second *Aliens* movie, "My programming makes it impossible for me to harm a human being. Keep them away from me."

His OCD? What a hilarious excuse. No one with OCD has ever committed a crime? And he says, "anyone who knows me." John, anyone who knows you knows you're a liar. And you are fully capable of bilking people out of money.

In the short time I had any kind of friendly relationship with Stuttering John, I saw him take advantage of so many people financially. So many people told me stories like, "Oh, yeah. Stuttering John, from *The Howard Stern Show*." He'd call up and go, "Hey, you want to catch up and get something to eat, man?" And every time, out with

John, it's you that's going to be forking over the money at the end of the day. He would never pull out a fucking dime.

John came over to my house to play poker with his buddy Mike, who is now my buddy Mike. John, of course, is dead money—he can't play for shit. He's just too fucking stupid to play poker. So, he needed more money, and he made Mike drive him to an ATM to take money out of Mike's account.

John has never picked up a bill for anything. When he taped his show from my studio in Manhattan, my staff had to come in and work his show, and we gave him the airtime, and this motherfucker didn't even tip. He didn't even give the guys a few bucks for their time. And he drank every fucking bit of alcohol that was in our fridge, and then just walked out and got pissed when it was brought up. He actually got belligerent at the fact that we would dare bring up that he's a cheap chiseling motherfucker. Oh, are you kidding me?

Anytime I hear that fucker get brought up on *Who Are These Podcasts?* I think, "This would be a great character." And I say it all the time: "This Stuttering John babbling buffoon character on your screen is brilliant—it's a brilliant take on an idiot doing a podcast." Unfortunately for John, he's not a made-up character. He *is* that guy. He literally is a buffoon. And there he is for the whole world to see him lying about so many things.

And here's my take on John's personal life. He has an ex-wife and three kids. Two of his kids are adults, and the youngest one is seventeen. So, we'll leave the last one alone, because he's still a kid. But one of his adult kids was born a girl and decided to transition to being a boy. Transgender. So brave.

I don't know how John has done it, but he seems to have scrubbed every picture of his daughter, now his son, off the internet. He probably tries his best to keep that shit off of there. But what a cute girl she was. I know there was a picture from her prom, where she and her girlfriend were crowned queens of the prom, and it was supposed to be like a groundbreaking achievement because they were both lesbians. And then she decided she didn't want to be a lesbian. She wanted to be a dude.

And here's what I think: because Stuttering John was such a poor parent, such a nonexistent father, this lovely girl (now boy) was screaming for some type of attention that she/he wasn't getting. John would rather be the goofy guy making $30,000 a year on *The Howard Stern Show* or being the joke on *The Tonight Show* than spend actual quality time with his fucking family.

So, the girl, starved of fatherly love and attention, goes, "Can you cut my tits off? Can you please just cut my tits off, and we'll try to fabricate some kind of proxy cock? And I'll be a boy now."

Back in the *Howard Stern* days, John would say "nigger" and "retard" and everything. He would make jokes about Robin Quivers for her race. He did some song parodies with "nigger" in them. He'd say "retard" all the time. This is who John is.

Now when your daughter decides to become a boy, because she's attention-starved due to her fucking nonexistent father, you have to do something. Because at some point in your life, you're probably gonna start looking back and go, "Hmm, maybe I've screwed the pooch here. Maybe this is all my fault."

So, John becomes this insanely, unreasonably left-wing mental patient. Remember, this is the same guy who dropped N-bombs and constantly used the word "retard." He was just a nasty Long Island piece of shit. And yes, we all fall into that category, man. It's the Long Island Piece of Shit category. Mostly, you know, a conservative kind of angry. But then he's like, "How can I win my daughter's/son's love back?" And to do that, he decides to become one of the most irrational left-wing people you'll ever see. "B-B-Biden's doing a great job!" Oh, is he really, John?

"D-d-dotard. They're there for the d-d-dotard! The GQP." He's got all of his little political catchphrases. He honestly fancies himself a political pundit. He thinks that people tune in to his show to see his clever take on the world of politics. Who's on today? Some congressman you've done no research on? Someone whose name you don't even know, nor what they stand for? Is that your guest?

And it's not that you can't do the research, John; the material is out there. You're just not motivated. And you're probably stupid. Much like Opie. Look, I'm sorry. I think the society we live in, and the one that we've lived in for quite a few years now, doesn't like to address the fact that some people are just stupid. And there is nothing they can do about it. There's no drug. There's no cure. There's no practice. No workout. There's nothing that can change stupidity. And some people are just stupid. John is one of them. And Opie is one of them. Owen Benjamin might not be stupid. In fact, I think he's very clever. But he is, in my opinion, another grifter.

Stuttering John would get very angry at my tweets. And of course, he would retweet mine, with left-wing organizations attached. Here's one of his tweets: "Dear GLAAD, Bullies Out, RAIN and Twitter Support. This person is bullying and harassing me and my transgender child on social media. His name is Anthony Cumia, a criminal and POC. This is one of his tweets where he is engaging in this despicable hateful behavior." I hope you read that in John's retarded, stuttering voice.

So, he knew that this lambasting from me was coming. A lot of people knew that I'd be going on my show and social media, and now using this book, to call out this fucking idiot for what he is. And the worst part for John is, what is he going to do? Is he going to call Erock and get him to tell me to be quiet?

Are you going to call Garrett and Drew, John? Maybe you could offer them some money and they'll just hit the off switch in my studio, and that'll be it. Or are you going to sic GLAAD on me? What is GLAAD going to do? I would gladly have GLAAD protests outside my studio as I walk in, so I could call them every name in the book as I go up and do my show. Do you understand, John, that some of us just don't give a fuck anymore? That we've already been backed into a corner and built up the ability to speak our minds and call out motherfucking pieces of shit like you? Do you understand?

Or are you going to hit up Twitter support? Are they going to cancel my account? Grow up. Who else are you calling, John? Your lawyer? Are you going to sue me? Like I said, sue away. I will not entertain your lawsuit. Your little attempts at scaring me on social media are not going to stop me.

And I feel bad for your poor family too. Look, my own dad wasn't the best provider, but he was a good guy to his kids—you know, loving. He was able to listen to us; he gave me some good advice over the years. I spent time in California with him riding horses and doing man things. John, on the other hand, is one of those weekend warrior sort of dads. They get divorced, and they just say, "Fuck it." And the reason they're divorced, by the way, is that they were ignoring their family. Then they continue to ignore them, but they talk like they are such supportive pillars in their families.

Dude, did you forget that we've heard everything about you? You are a public figure. You did build up some fame. You're in that category where people are allowed to talk about you and your personal life. Yes, they are. And we saw it happening, John. We saw it happening on *The Howard Stern Show*—Howard would call out what a piece of shit you were and are: "Hero of the stupid. You're a hero of the stupid." You've been a babbling buffoon your entire career, and you've lost your family. Lost whatever money you might have made during the height of your career. And now you're begging for money for some very, very shady cancer charity. You said you'd collect the money on your account and then send it along. What a crock of shit.

All of that effort to send maybe one hundred dollars for chemo? What's a hundred bucks going to get you? That's like going to a gas station and saying, "Give me a dollar's worth of regular."

I just don't know how he thinks that shit is even legit. How the fuck does this idiot think anyone but another idiot like himself is going to believe that? Why did the money have to go through so many channels, John? Why did you have to go through a third party instead of just giving it straight to the chemo patient?

This is like watching fucking *Scarface* with the money-counting machines and watching where it's going. In my opinion, it sounds like money laundering. Jesus Christ, the guy won't launder his underwear because there might be fucking roaches in it. Yet he might be laundering a hundred dollars. If you really had any fucking morality or empathy or sympathy, John, you would have sent them a donation out of your own money and never mentioned it on your show. That's what a person who actually cares about people does. They don't put it out on their show, trying to fucking get publicity or money.

I think that you're a lying crock of shit, John. I believe you took that money for yourself, that it never went to a chemo patient or anybody else.

John went on to say that because of his inability to do wrong, he can't even bring himself to take free stuff at hotels. He said his OCD prevents him from stealing at all. Does the hilarity ever stop? He's like, "I don't take anything. The soap, the shampoo? Never saw it, never even used it. Laundry? Never did it."

This babbling buffoon actually said he doesn't take things from hotels. Everyone takes something, whether it's soap or shampoo. Has he ever taken a towel? I doubt it. You'd have to take a shower to use a towel, and I don't think he's ever showered. And then his example of how he can't steal due to OCD is never taking anything from a hotel? Brilliant.

He's like Ricky Gervais' character from the British version of *The Office*, David Brent. It's a brilliantly moronic out-of-touch character that Ricky plays, but Ricky is a smart, really funny guy in real life. David Brent is just a character. Unlike Stuttering John, who lives his entire fucking act.

John also likes to portray himself as some great legal mind and the winner of many lawsuits, because he once sued Sharon Stone's bodyguard and settled for $30,000, which John counts as a win. I'm sure Sharon Stone was really nervous trying to scrape up thirty large. Then you have taxes, and then what percentage does the lawyer get? I think this happened in 1996, during the *Stern* years, so he would have had the corporation's legal team representing him. Which makes sense, since John isn't going to pay for attorneys' fees out of pocket.

Technically, I guess John did "win" that lawsuit. So, he won one lawsuit in the previous century. He hasn't won a single lawsuit in this century, let alone many.

Threatening to sue me is so fucking childish. It reminds me of when someone stands on the curb in front of their house and tells someone they're mad at, "Get off my property." And then the other person goes, "The curb is the government's property, not your private property."

That's how John's lawsuits are—ridiculous. I guarantee you that Sharon Stone never even heard about the lawsuit against her bodyguard. You can ask her, and she'd be like, "What? Who?" And whether it was her own full-time bodyguard or a hired service for that night or that day, the bodyguard's company has insurance. When they're sued, all they do is go, "Well, we'll settle. Offer thirty thousand and see if they'll take it."

But John is like, "I s-s-sued S-S-Sharon Stone." Nope, she's never fucking heard of it. Holy shit. You sued an insurance company for a security company, John, and they gave you $30,000 to go away. Again, he's just so full of shit. Can you picture it? "I would like to act as my own attorney. I call to the stand S-S-Sharon S-S-Stone. Cross your legs, crossing your legs and across again, ex post facto, and atheist core puzzle stuttering job. I took Sharon Stone for thirty grand, and fifty percent goes to the lawyer, so that's fifteen grand." With other fees subtracted, the guy walked away with nothing even close to a typical appearance fee. It was like when he used to do an appearance at Hard Rock or something.

Even the $30,000 sounds like it was their lowball bid. They were probably like, "Oh, he'll definitely say a hundred grand after we offer him thirty." But he was like, "Thirty grand? Fuck yes! I'll take it!" It's like when Kramer on *Seinfeld* just wanted to be in a Marlboro ad, or get a bunch of free cafe lattes as compensation for the hot coffee that spilt on his lap. That's exactly who John is. Again, a brilliant fake character that isn't fake. He's an actual human that you can watch on his show.

This is a great plug for you, by the way, John. We give you so many plugs for your show, whether it's *Who Are These Podcasts?* with Karl, *The Uncle Rico Show* with Shuli and Bob Levy, my own show, or other podcasts that make more money off of you than you make for yourself. We're all like, "Holy fuck, is he for real?" But John really has to be filtered through something like one of the shows mentioned, because he is just the worst.

He is so litigious—he sees everything he does through the prism of a lawsuit. He thinks he's being careful on his show by not using my name and saying things like, "Maybe you bit your girlfriend or whatever you did. I don't know." Like he's trying to keep plausible deniability. John, say what you want, I'm not going to sue you. I'm not an idiot. Say my name. Call me an asshole, call me criminal, call me a liar, call me fucking whatever you want. I will never sue you. Do whatever you want. I'm fine with it. But if you talk, then I'll talk. I'll make you look like the jerk-off you are. But you're on eggshells when it comes to me, like, "Who's that guy? I don't know. I don't know what he did."

The clip he showed on his show was of Dani Brand and me having an argument. She smacked me upside the head and cocked back again, and I grabbed her hand or wrist, and gently bit her hand and went, "Don't touch me." That was it. There you go. That's how I beat a girl's hand. Got it? I've said that many times on my show. So, if you don't already know about it, you're just not doing your research.

He's so stupid. He doesn't even know what constitutes something I might be able to sue him for. For instance, you can call people racist. And I'm definitively stating that Stuttering John is a racist. There, I said it. Why is this guy peeking around corners and tiptoeing? Just say it: "You're a racist." There, that's how it's done.

Hey, John, do you or Opie want to keep thinking that Patrice O'Neal hated me and thought I was a racist? I laugh at this all the time, because I get a lot of social media posts saying, "Patrice would be embarrassed of you. Patrice would be so pissed. Patrice wouldn't talk to you." Anyone who thinks they knew what Patrice was going to say or think about anything is way out of their league. No one could figure out where that guy was going. Patrice was all over the place. He was such a unique mind, and if you think you could've figured him out or that you were five steps ahead of him, shut the fuck up. And anyone who assumes what type of relationship me and Patrice had on and off the air is full of shit. I know what kind of relationship we had. My friends and family know too, because they were around when Patrice was at my house or the studio.

Patrice and I had a very cool, fun, funny, sometimes adversarial relationship. Some of the arguments we had were race-based, but we had so much in common. We both found the same shit funny. And you know, Opie's shit talk about how Patrice thought I was a racist is his way of trying to get at me. The truth is that Patrice hated Opie, because

Opie made him sit out in the waiting room while no one was even inside.

But getting back to Stuttering John and his cancer scam, John insists he has a paper trail for all the monies he took for it. First of all, it's not a paper trail; it's just paperwork. A paper trail is all the documentation that leads from one thing to another, and it can involve other people. Second, if it were actually a paper trail, then that sounds a little nefarious anyway, because a paper trail always involves something bad. Like, "Oh, they left a paper trail. It's going to be easy to fucking pick them up and prove their guilt."

John also claims he sent the "beloved chatter" an iPad mini. You might have heard him refer to it on his show. He did a whole thing on how he can't believe that he's been called out as a crook when he just wants to help people. And he goes, "You know this guy to beloved chatter needed an iPad. And I, out of my own money, I sent them a mini iPad." Why say that you did, John? Why say it on air? There's no reason to bring up your charitable fucking contributions unless you're trying to cover for something underhanded.

About the chemo money, John goes, "The first payment was sent, then I will send the next one out on the first of the month, even though I don't get paid from YouTube till the twenty-first, but I'll still do it anyway. So, this person could have the money and could put it towards what they need."

Another ridiculous statement by John. He's going to send the money for chemo on the first even though he doesn't get the money from YouTube until later. When, supposedly, he's been collecting money from innocent people for this very reason all along? Plus, is the supposed cancer patient just sitting there with the chemo tube waiting for John's money to turn the chemo on? No, of course not. They bill you. If you don't have insurance, they'll give you the treatments and then bill you, and you then have to come up with the money or file for bankruptcy, or you've got to do something else. Does he even fucking know how anything works in the healthcare system?

Holy mother of Christ on a pony. He's so dumb. So, he's going to send the money right away so they can get that chemo drip started and the person doesn't die. John thinks he's saving lives.

John also claimed on his show that it might not be worth his time to sue me. "Now I don't know how much money you have left on that failed network of yours," he said. "So, uh, you know, I don't even know if it's worth suing you." More hilarity ensues.

Doesn't this idiot think I have more than $35,000? Like, he sued Sharon Stone and was fine with $35,000. Now you must assume, John—come on—that I have a little more than $35,000. I literally won that at the Borgata. The last time I was there, I won twice that amount at the blackjack tables. So, if it's $35,000 and I have to pay you in

$5,000 Borgata strapped stacks, I could do that. I got you covered, John.

But to spew, "I don't know how much money you got left with that failed-over-eight-years company, over-nine-years company, over eight years in Manhattan, doing podcasts, doing comedy shows"? Holy shit. Talk about lacking self-awareness. How long do I have to do something before these trolls or whatever you want to call them have to go, "I guess we can't really use that line of attack anymore. Fuck." The fact of the matter is, we've been doing this for nine years. Eight years of that has been from our own studio in Manhattan.

I'd probably be worth suing, John. Please. I am waiting for a process server to come through my studio door and hand me the Stuttering John Melendez lawsuit. I'd probably read the lawsuit on the air. I want to laugh at it. I want to post it all over the place, and I'd never show up in court, because you're a fucking joke.

John also thinks things are slander when they aren't. He's a public figure. He's doing things, and people are talking about them and calling them out. You want slander, John? Here's some slander for you: "I might have seen Stuttering John fucking a homeless guy in the mouth outside an empty gas station." There, that might be slanderous. Do you get the difference? When I say I most likely believe that Stuttering John is stealing money with a bogus cancer charity, that's not really slander because he's kind of got to show that he's not. And I most likely believe he is.

But let's move on now, to how John, in his lunatic left-wing mind, likes to attack Donald Trump and my support of him. Here's a bit of a rant from the stuttering thief's own mouth, from his show: "You want to talk about character? Okay, let's talk about character. Because I would never steal from a charity like the Trump kids did. Yeah, but you know that president you support, you pock-faced animal? Yeah, that president? Yeah, yeah. How many people did he stiff? How many bankruptcies did he declare? So that's the one that you worship? And then attack a good guy like me for wanting to help people? You fucking animal."

It's very, very interesting when he talks about Trump like that. He's so dumb and so broke. I feel bad for him. I mean, anyone who is his age and has nothing has to be petrified when they look at the future. They have nothing in the game. He doesn't even understand how much better Trump was for him than Biden is. The stock market keeps going down and down under this administration. This idiot doesn't understand that if you had any skin in the game whatsoever, you'd have appreciated the four years Trump was in office.

If Trump were still in office, I'd have my money invested in something sound, and it would be making gains of 20 percent a year. But no. And John is so dumb and so brainwashed that he has to trash-talk Trump to try to win back his liberal daughter/son's love. He just can't fucking fathom that Donald Trump was way better for the basic American workingman than pretty much any president, arguably, and was absolutely better than Biden has been.

We're losing money hand over fist, and this dummy just can't understand it. He keeps saying that Trump's kids steal and talking about Trump's bankruptcies. Yeah, the reality of the situation is that if you have a fuckload of businesses over the years, some are going to be extremely successful, and others will fall by the wayside. It's called taking chances. It's called betting on yourself. You know, it's called being in the game. John, you have had only failures.

Trump has had his bankruptcies, which you could consider business failures, but they're offset by an amazingly successful life. What the fuck do you have, John? You have a family who cannot fucking stand you. A career that…I don't even know what it is. Did you quit stand-up comedy because some people gave you a little bit of shit, or because no one was laughing? You couldn't book a gig? The club owner would hear your name and go, "Oh Stuttering John from *The Howard Stern Show*." And then book you, and then when it got close to showtime would go, "Yeah, we sold no tickets." So, John, you quit the game because of trolls and lack of talent and lack of ability to fill a room. Fuck you, John. Fuck your mother. Fuck her too.

John has nothing in his life but his few "glory days" to look back on, which *Who Are These Podcasts?* and *The*

Uncle Rico Show dissect, discuss, and laugh at beautifully. Hell, shitting on John has become an industry. There's a whole community around it. There've even been fan conventions based solely on his idiocy. And all of these shows have one thing in common: they're making more money goofing off John than John can make for himself. Long live the Dabbleverse!

Fuck you, John. Now go home and g-g-get your fucking sh-sh-shine box.

BILL BURR AND OTHER BITCHES
● ● ● ● ● ● ● ●

I THINK MOST OF YOU will remember hearing about a little tiff that I was involved in a few months ago with some old friends of mine at the Comedy Cellar. One day after wrapping up my show at 6 p.m., I went downtown to the Fat Black Pussycat club to see my good friend Jimmy Norton. I loved it. Love him. We're inseparable.

To no one's surprise, I may have had a few drinks that evening before I proceeded to make my way over to the Comedy Cellar—which, of course, is the iconic gathering place for comedians on MacDougal Street in the Village. Now, coincidentally, the night before this little tiff took place, a Patrice O'Neal benefit happened. (Yeah, I was at a couple of those benefits in the past until I became something called persona non grata and was not invited back. It was a personal thing between Bill Burr and his wife and me. It's not as sordid as it sounds.)

So, I went to the Cellar, and Amy Schumer was there too. I saw her walk in, and I think she went right downstairs with her security guy. Now this next question is for old *O&A* fans: Who do you think might have been working security for Amy Schumer? Take a wild guess. Could it be "Ginger Ale" Joe? "Frappuccino" Frank? Nope. Those people don't exist. It was none other than Club Soda Kenny.

So, Kenny walks in, and Amy is in front of him. So, he probably can't see much of the club ahead of him. Because she's so fucking fat. Get it? So, I see Kenny and I try to get his attention. I go, "Kenny? Kenny?" He finally looks at me, turns his head, and keeps walking. And I keep going, "Kenny? Kenny?" Nothing. I mean: Totally. Fucking. Ignored.

Well, he's a security guy, and I get that part of it, but working security for somebody should not make you obligated to despise the people your client despises, should it? Especially if you've had a very close relationship over decades. I was Kenny's client many times myself. I was mostly Keith the Cop's client, but Kenny was like Opie's security guy. He was always around, and he became somewhat of a known character on the show.

Since he was mainly Opie's guy, maybe there is still some resentment brewing, so I'm just like, "Alright, look,

I can understand that." Now Amy? Amy does not like me at this point. I bashed the shit out of her, as we all should. She's a Schumer, for fuck's sake. Like Chuck Schumer. She's constantly bashing our Second Amendment rights.

So, I'm like, "Okay, no big deal," and I continue to have a few more drinks. And as I've already said, the Patrice O'Neal Benefit Comedy Concert took place the night before, and big-name comedians who performed at it are still in town. Now, I ask you, who puts on this benefit every year? Well, it's none other than Bill fucking Burr.

Well, if Bill Burr is in town and all these comics who performed at the benefit are in town, where would they go in New York City? They'd go to a familiar place where they honed their comedy chops, and that place would be the Comedy Cellar.

So, Bill Burr walks in the joint and I'm sitting there, and I see him, and I'm not going to be a dick. (It was actually Bill Burr, by the way, not just someone who looked like him.) I'm going to go over there to be sincere and try my best to, as the comedian Bobby Kelly said, "bury this shit with Burr." I saw Bobby in Chicago when he was opening for Louie C.K. He said, "Can you bury this shit with Burr?"

So, I'm like, "Look, we're both here. Let me take Bobby's advice and see if I can't bury this shit with Burr. I'll try it." I walk up to Bill's table and look at him. He's sitting down, and I put my knee on a chair to get on an equal level. "Billy, what's up?" I say. "How are you doing?" Now,

I'm starting to think maybe this was not the best idea. He responds with, "Dude." But it's not a warm "hey, dude." It's more like, "*Dude!* What the fuck?" It's an angry, bitchy "dude." Kind of in the same tone of voice when he talks about white women. With utter disdain and disgust.

He then says to me, "Why the fuck are you talking to me, after all the shit you said about my wife?" I say, "Bill, first of all, the fans are the ones that kicked that whole fucking thing off. I never said anything…" Well, I don't get many more words out before Bill's security, who happens to be none other than the aforementioned Club Soda Kenny, makes an appearance. Now, another question for the old *O&A* fans reading this: Who else does Club Soda Kenny do security for? Yes, that's right. Lil' Jimmy Norton.

But as I said, I saw Jim just a few hours prior. I spoke to him, and he was great. Funny-as-fuck show. He's one of the loves of my life, Jim Norton. So, I know it's not really an issue that Kenny is doing security for Jimmy, because Kenny knows Jimmy and I are dear friends.

But what does Kenny do when I approach Bill and try to bury the shit? He throws me out of the Comedy Cellar.

Oh, yeah. It happened. He literally chest-bumped me out of the fucking place. Evidently, I am not worthy of burying any shit with Bill Burr. And by the way, that's why I never previously tried to bury the shit with Bill Burr. In my drunken haze that night at the Comedy Cellar, it seemed like a good idea. I was hearing the words of Bobby

Kelly echoing in my head: "You have to bury this shit with Burr, dude. Come on, dude."

But Kenny, the guy I fucking spent years with when he was one of our security guys, chest-bumped me and physically removed me, saying in that stupid voice of his, "Go. Go."

Now, my fans know that when I'm drinking, and especially when I'm drunk, I turn into a magnanimous fucking dickface…. I'm kidding. See? That's part of the joke. I don't get drunk and belligerent. I'm not a belligerent guy. Especially when I'm trying to bury shit. I didn't go, "Oh, big star Billy Burr, Mr. *Mandalorian*, you're probably 'womandalorian' or 'fagdalorian,' anything but 'man.'" I didn't say that. And then I was physically eight-sixed out of the joint by Club Soda.

I was beside myself. Pissed beyond words. Just stewing over the fact that this fucking guy we supported and employed for years, and enjoyed the company of for years, would treat me like I was just another piece of shit in the way of one of his paychecks. Just another piece of garbage that needed to be removed because his current employer might have been getting upset that I would dare try to bury the shit with him.

I am absolutely fucking disgusted. Fuck Bill Burr up his fucking ginger, black wife's ass.

Fuck Club Soda Kenny. He's, he's…I actually don't know what to say about him. But the hypocrisy of Club

Soda Kenny doing security for Bill, and of Bill hiring him as his security, is astounding. I've heard Kenny say shit that would have the talking heads spinning as far as racial and gay humor goes. And believe me, I laughed harder than anybody. I loved it. And I don't think anyone should be upset with that. But don't fucking even try to make this like I am so repugnant to the likes of Billy Burr. That it's acceptable for a guy I spent years working at different gigs with, and have paid money to, to treat me like garbage. Because I've said things that rub people the wrong way?

Fuck off. All of them can just fuck off.

So, a few weeks after this latest Bill Burr incident, Erock comes over to Sullivan's bar across the street from our studio, where I usually have a bite to eat and a drink—maybe do a shot or two with Geno—and do prep before the show at 4 p.m. And he comes over to my table with his cell phone in hand and says people are sending clips of me from when I was gaming in my apartment late at night, live-streaming it, and saying mean, horrible things. He says a bunch of comics have been passing it around and commenting on it, etc. Now, I love Erock, and I appreciate that he has come over to me and let me know about it, and I tell him that I appreciate it, but I also tell him something that I want everyone, and I mean everyone, to know. Which is, I don't give a fuck. I really, truly do not give one single fuck.

For me, there's a pretty simple question to ask: Why the fuck are any of these people, especially the comics, having this holier-than-thou attitude about what I talk about? What the fuck have they done for me in the last ten years, since we've been doing Compound Media? What have they done to help grow my show or grow Compound Media or anything else? Even when I was biting my tongue and holding back a little on certain topics, I was totally honest with people. I always have been. When Keith the Cop was there, he tried to keep a tight rein on me. And I'm not saying this in a bad way, but it was in Keith's best interest when he was working here to make the place somewhere where we could have guests like, you know, actors, pundits, newsmakers, big-name comics from New York, and various other interesting people. But they weren't fucking coming on anyway.

Well, how about attracting sponsors? We have got to talk about getting big sponsors. And they, too, weren't coming on anyway. I had a DVD sponsor. I had ManGrate. I had some flower companies for a little while, and maybe some teddy bears. We do have the jeweler Steven Singer and I love Steven Singer; everyone else hates him, but I love him. We have gold, which is just an element of planet Earth. Thank God gold isn't emotional.

But I have had it with these pretentious, self-indulgent, holier-than-thou, judgmental douchebags that call themselves comedians. Comics—funny, funny guys, right? I've had it with these fucks. How do you go onstage and do comedy and then go around acting all judgmentally with other people? First of all, most comics are borderline socio-paths, as I've said several times, and sexual deviants and fucking drug addicts and alcoholics and whatever. And then the likes of them are going to judge me, Anthony Cumia, because of nothing more than what I say?

You want to call me racist, homophobic, whatever. Why? Because I'm talking about stuff? I've never gone out and done anything to people who I've had a problem with. Like I've never actually *done* anything about the way a specific group of people acts in a civil society. I've only talked about it.

And the way I get judged for just talking about something is absurd. Some comics literally want to punch me in the head and punch me in the face and beat the shit out of me and prevent me from being in a club or some other venue. So, is that the logical, reasonable response to me just voicing an opinion?

I've been doing shows for almost thirty years. That's a long time to be in front of a microphone. And all I've done is speak out about the things I've seen, lived, heard, and done, and convey that to the audience in, hopefully, some type of entertaining way.

I've never incited or asked for violence. On the *O&A* show, Jimmy and I made what were obviously jokes about domestic violence and things like that. And people are free to do that in this country—make such obviously ridiculous jokes that no reasonable person would think they were real. It falls under the protection of the First Amendment.

Jokes like that are few and far between, however. I also have opinions, of course, which for the most part are based on things I've seen, heard, read, and experienced. People are entitled to their opinions. And some idiots are driven to the point where they want to physically assault me over them? They think they can judge what's right and decent in the world and mete out their brand of justice on me? They can go screw themselves!

This kind of stuff totally fits 2023 America, where everything is now completely fuck-ass backwards. Someone wants to get violent with me for joking and voicing opinions, thinking I'm a piece of shit for merely saying what I'm saying, and they're not a piece of shit for wanting to beat the shit out of me?

But I'll tell you another thing. I'll go wherever the fuck I want. I don't stay away from places just because someone there might have a problem with me. I'll walk right in, just like with the Comedy Cellar and Bill Burr. What really pissed me off about that was the physicality of it and how impersonal it was. I've known Kenny forever, and he could have just said, "Hey, hey, look, look, this isn't the time or place. Just go back to your seat." But no, he had to immediately get physical by chest-bumping me out of the place, no conversation at all.

These fucking comics would just love you to believe they're so amazingly open about everything. You know, "comics are the new philosophers"–type bullshit. Comics are just as big fucking business-oriented hypocrites as the shit-fucking elected officials in politics. They have their little cliques and groups, and they have to adhere to the rules of their little group. Like, some guy won't let you into a club or a show because some other guy doesn't like you. And if you are friendly with some guy, then some other guy won't work for you. What a crock of shit. But, yeah, comics are all fucking tough guys, right? Look out, we're rebel philosophers. Oh, yeah, "I got my microphone and my stage, and I'm a rebel…." No, you're just a faggot.

You're not tough. You're not rebellious. You're not even real people. You're a bunch of corporate-run puppets that march in line and go along with whatever the fuck is the current agenda. And you'll kowtow to whatever it is you think people need to hear out of you. Make me laugh, jester. Make me laugh, puppet. That's what you fucks are.

And the second anyone says anything that's not on the agenda, they're persona non grata. You think the shit I say is offensive? Then don't talk to me. I don't give a fuck. Don't you understand? You of all people, comedians, should understand that I have my own fucking thing. And I'll talk about what I believe in and what I do and what I think. And I deserve threats of violence for that? What the fuck is that about?

If you're a fan of my show, you know I'm referring at this point to a comedian named Godfrey. He's black. I don't know a lot about him, don't know how he's faring in the comedy world, but I've heard the name before. And I have to be honest: if this fuck Godfrey is going on Chad Zumock's show, he cannot be doing that well.

And Chad Zumock, by the way, should be bowing down to everyone from me to Karl from *Who Are These Podcasts?* to Kevin Brennan, Bob Levy, Shuli Egar, and anyone else who has mentioned his unknown fucking name over the past year or so. Chad will go, "Hey, my viewers are up. My Patreon numbers are up." Look, Chad, in my opinion, you're a retarded fuck, but do you really think your viewer numbers are up because people are finally seeing your amazing talent? Are you thinking, "Finally, what took so long for people to see I'm a world-class comedian"? You dumb fuck. It's because everyone is making fun of you. Because it's likely a lot of people think you might be an unfunny retard. And a lying unfunny retard at that.

You haven't hit this amazing crossroads in life and chosen the road to being actually funny. Hasn't happened. So really, Chad, you should probably get on your little fucking knees and pray every night that people like me continue to talk about your dumb fucking unfunny lying ass, please.

But I digress. I was talking about Godfrey, and him being on that douchebag show speaks volumes. So, he goes on Chad's show, and now he's sticking his fucking nose into shit that doesn't concern him, like what happened at the Comedy Cellar. So, Bill Burr doesn't want to talk to me because he's offended and pissed. He wants to beat me up. It's personal; it involves his wife. And now the whole thing involves Club Soda Kenny. But you know who it doesn't involve? Godfrey. You want to inject yourself into situations where real-people big boys are talking to each other, Godfrey? Feel free. But don't think I'm not going to mention that you really have no business in the conversation at all.

But Godfrey felt the need to comment on what happened. And again, understand that everything I've done that has pissed anyone off is purely words on a show or on social media. But Godfrey has threatened me with physical violence over what I've said and the fact that I tried to bury the shit with Bill Burr at the Comedy Cellar. He went on Chad's show and said if I ever came to the Cellar again, I'd get beat up.

Look, if anyone at a club threatened *him* with violence, they'd be thrown out of the club and called an asshole. But just because I'm speaking my thoughts, which he happens to disagree with, he thinks that should be met with physical violence? Oh, yes. Godfrey threatened me that if I came into a certain free, open establishment, he'd beat me up. What is this, Godfrey's Comedy Cellar down in the Village? No, it's not. They're not gonna change the sign to "Godfrey's Comedy Cellar." I do fully expect the owner,

Noam, to change the sign at some point. But it isn't going to have fucking Godfrey's name on it.

So, here's a little excerpt of what Godfrey had to say about me on dumb-shit Chad Zumock's show: "First of all, you want to squash a beef? It's all phony. You want to come and squash the beef, about you dogging his wife on public platforms, and then you're going to come to a dead black man's benefit? Go fuck yourself. Get the fuck out and bless him ever come to the Cellar again. Or you get beat the fuck up. So, Anthony, keep it moving, dude."

Obviously, he's talking about Bill Burr and that I talked shit about Bill's wife on my platform. But here's the thing: I didn't talk shit about Bill Burr's wife. It was the listeners that were initially responsible for doing this. Here's what actually happened. When I was on SiriusXM, I spoke out about how that black woman had assaulted me in Times Square, and then I jumped to violence in the black community. (And by the way, I walked away from that situation in Times Square. I didn't return the violence.) And Sirius summarily fired me for my "racist" diatribe, which is hilarious because now all anyone talks about is the violence going on and the need to stop it. But back then, the focus was on my "racist" diatribe.

When the listeners of the *Opie & Anthony* show, and then subsequently of my own program on Compound Media, found out what had happened, they started jumping on the comics to find out which were supporting me and which were alienating me because of my supposed racism and racist rant. And this didn't involve just Bill Burr. Holy fuck, every single comic that had ever done the *Opie & Anthony* show got a message from our fans on social media or what have you, asking them if they supported me. I appreciated the shit out of it. I liked the fact that the fans were motivated to want to know who was still friendly and who was running for the hills. I understood why some would run for the hills though. I've said many times that I understood if some comics wanted to back away.

A perfect example is one of my best friends, Adam Ferrara. Adam is a clean-as-a-whistle fucking comic. I don't even think he says the word "fuck" onstage. He's had TV deals and been on a bunch of shows, like *Rescue Me* with Denis Leary and *Nurse Jackie* with Edie Falco, and was a host on the American version of *Top Gear* on the History channel. The guy has been around.

Look, I understood the situation. I wasn't going to approach Adam and say, "Hey, man, come on over here and support me." No, I got it. I understood the motivation behind why he wouldn't. I'm not stupid. I wouldn't want anyone to put their entire career and life on the line just to make me go, "Well, thank you, minion. You've supported me. Now, go get a job in construction." Adam is one of my best friends, as I said, and still, I understand why he wouldn't support me.

So, that's not even the real point here. The point is that the fans called out the comics who were perceived to not be supporting me. And they said terrible things and logical things and also sometimes talked about things that never actually happened. I get it. That's how the fans work. And as a guest of the show for many years, Bill Burr should have fucking known that fact very well.

I had nothing to do with the fans going after Bill's black wife when Bill did not support me after my firing in 2014. But he thought I should have done something about it. I saw Bill a few years ago in Los Angeles when I was promoting my first book, and he said, "You didn't even, like, stick up for her or publicly say that the fans should stop doing what they're doing."

Now again, there are fans and then there are *fans*. As a guest on the show and doing *O&A* stand-up concerts for many years, where you'd interact with our fans and see them up close, you know first-fucking-hand that *O&A* fans were way different than any other fans in the country, Bill. They were literally nicknamed "The Pests." We used to make them viciously attack our competitors' websites by saying, "Please don't attack this website." We used to make them call the show and make guests cry by saying, "Please call in with serious questions only! Serious questions only!" And we did it with a constant wink.

I truly thought the best thing for me to do in the situation with Bill's wife was not say anything, as long as Bill and his wife knew that I had nothing to do with it. These are the same fans, by the way, that have thrown monkey wrenches into my career over the years as well as the careers of my brother, my sisters, my family, and my friends. I've had to deal with The Pests fucking around and getting my gigs canceled and whatnot.

So again, it was not my intention to go after Bill's wife, but rather the intention of these monsters we all somehow built over the years. It is what it is. And I'm sorry about it, but that's what all of us involved with O&A have had to deal with. It's part of the cost for what we got out of it—very good careers. The fans were rabid. And they came to all those shows and saw those comics perform, and then they went back to their home cities or whatnot, and they continued to listen to the show every day. So, it worked out pretty well for everybody who had thick enough skin to take the abuse from those fans.

For some reason—and I think I know what that reason is—Bill wasn't ready to accept any abuse from fans. However, at that time I thought he might have been ready to accept it. So, as I mentioned earlier, when I went out to Los Angeles about five years ago to do shows to promote my first book, I met with Bill to see if we could smooth things over. Then maybe we could somehow work together on a podcast or cohosting shows, or I could go to the Patrice O'Neal benefit—shit like that.

Well, I sit down in a club with him. And he just gets right to the point and goes, "Look, my wife is very upset, and I can't work with you anymore. I can't do anything with you anymore." And it's cordial. I'm like, "Alright, alright. I get it." And that's it. He said this before I could even explain the situation from my end. Then he goes, "My wife didn't even want me coming here to meet with you tonight." So, he tipped his hand a little there. I'm thinking, "Look, it's a lot easier to tell Anthony that you can't work with him anymore than it is to go home to a pissed-off wife." Yes, it is easier. Am I supposed to respect that decision? The answer is: no, I don't.

Again, the whole situation with Bill's wife wasn't based on something I said. It was based on the fans having said what they said, and they were being really fucking nasty. They're pieces of shit. I get it. But that's the fan base we raised. We raised shitty children. Me and Opie were not good parents, especially with Uncle Bill, Uncle fucking Jimmy, Uncle Rich, Uncle Bobby, Uncle Nick, and Uncle Patrice in the family. We raised rambunctious offspring.

Over the years since it happened, I've heard things about my being an awful person, and my being a racist always comes up. And I honestly believe that this is at least partly because of Bill's wife's influence. I mean, look, she's a black woman. It's no secret, and she has a certain agenda, as most black people do when it comes to their history and people. And I don't know why that agenda exists or where it comes from. I don't think it's logical, and I don't think it's reasonable. But whatever. We all have to live with it.

Over the years, things got a lot more heated. I feel like a lot of people that Bill previously had brought onboard weren't coming on my show anymore because of him. Now, I don't know that for a fact. I also don't know if I was no longer welcome on Chip Chipperson's show because *The Chip Chipperson Podcast* started broadcasting on the podcast platform that Bill Burr has in Los Angeles. But I know what two plus two is.

I know how well-received my appearances on Chip Chipperson were. I know that those were some of the audience's favorite episodes. So, considering those two things, I might have to think that Bill might have said something to Chip about not wanting me to appear anywhere on his platform—just as there are people I wouldn't want to appear on my platform, even if it's just a video of them.

Since I don't know for sure, I would have liked to discuss it with Bill when I saw him sitting in the Comedy Cellar. I thought, "When am I going to get the opportunity again to be in the same room with this guy? It just doesn't happen anymore. So let me walk up, and I'll try." I didn't stand there. I didn't flex. I didn't go, "Hey, fucker. Let's take it outside." I was cordial. I said, "Hey, Bill. Can we talk for a minute?" No.

And again, I'm okay with that. I get it. I know he's not thinking, "Oh, look at this great guy, Anthony. I'll sit and talk with him." But the way Kenny removed me was way out of line, and it was not what you would think would have happened after I'd worked with both Bill and Kenny for so many years. At that point, I thought it was all on Kenny, really. But I don't know if Bill gave Kenny a sign somehow. Maybe Bill winked at Kenny, and Kenny's Frankenstein monster came out and removed me.

Anyway, getting back to stupid Godfrey. He had nothing to do with any of that. And while he's saying I shouldn't have walked up to Bill, he's simultaneously saying he'd walk up to me. Which is idiotic. You don't walk up to people you don't know. And Godfrey, you don't know me, and I don't know you, but you're ready to walk up to me if you see me in the Comedy Cellar and punch me in the face?

I was walking up to Bill simply to talk, and your response to that is threatening me? What a prime fucking example of the ass-backwards thinking that's going on right now. And Godfrey, you're a prime example of it. That's all I'm saying. Of course, you want to punch me, you fucker.

A black girl named Francine used to intern for us at the *O&A* show. Fans would remember Francine and her hilarious answers during trivia contests with her, Bobby Kelly, and Rich Vos. We would laugh as they would give the most moronic answers to very easy questions. For example, Francine thought that Louie Armstrong landed on the moon, instead of Neil. Ya know, great answers like that.

She's a sweetheart, a very funny, kind of dumb but, you know, lovable little Tutsi girl. She used to tell us that she was a Tutsi and not a Hutu—both of those being tribes in Rwanda, in case you didn't know. So, she'd talk about her Tutsi body and her Tutsi head. She made me laugh my ass off, the lovely Francine. I love her. She's fucking great. And about a week after Godfrey spewed his shit on Chad Zumock's show, Francine and I hit the town together for dinner and a few drinks. And where did we go to have said dinner and drinks? Yep, the Comedy Cellar. And I was praying to all the gods of Wakanda that Godfrey would be there so he could see me at the Cellar with a black woman. Unfortunately, he wasn't.

What would you have done, Godfrey? Would you have really walked up to an interracial couple sitting and enjoying a lovely dinner up in the Olive Tree above the Comedy Cellar, and punched the white guy in the face? Really? Is that what you were going to do? Punch me in the face in front of a beautiful, young African American woman? Feel free, Godfrey. Damn, how I wish you had been there that night. I would've just been hanging out and having a nice civil chitchat with the lovely Francine, maybe some of the other comics in there. And then whenever you felt the moment was right, you'd have punched me in the face. Oh, I would have gone right to Page Six and talked about how Godfrey's racist ass punched me, a white guy, just because I was on a date with a beautiful young Tutsi girl. Would you have liked that, Godfrey? I don't mess around. I make moves! That's what I do. I think things out. I come up with solutions.

Now let's turn to Godfrey's using the term "dead black man," as in, "a dead black man's benefit." His name was Patrice, Godfrey. You should probably know it, even though he never knew yours. Me and Patrice were friends. We were really friends, not just professional colleagues. We hung out. He'd come over to my house, and we had amazing talks and debates with each other on and off the air, because that fucker understood what I was about, and I understood what he was about. And we could be worlds apart on issues, and oftentimes we were. But Patrice never, ever threatened to punch me in the face, regardless of what the fuck I said. Never. He disagreed with me on so much shit but never disrespected anyone's ability and need to speak their mind.

That's a real comic. That's a brilliant man. That's someone you want in this world! Unfortunately, he's not here. And you are, Godfrey. How about that? You racist fuck!

OWEN
"FLAT EARTH"
BENJAMIN

● ● ● ●

I USED TO BE A fan of Owen Benjamin's, the comic and actor. For years. Even when people started calling him crazy and not supporting him, I was supporting him. This guy was one of the Hollywood people and was ensconced in that whole lifestyle, and then he decided, "I'm going to get a wife, and we're going to move into the woods of Idaho or Washington or upstate New York or wherever the fuck and raise a family and hunt and farm. And then from time to time, I'll just pop on one of my social media platforms and play piano and discuss shit."

How could anyone possibly hear about this, see someone go through that process of completely transitioning into a new lifestyle, and go, "Oh, what an asshole"? I absolutely could not. When I heard about what Owen was doing, all I thought was, "Holy fuck. That's awesome. Good for him." And I truly thought that, and that's what I said for years. In fact, prior to the summer of 2023, I challenge you to find a clip of me talking shit about Owen Benjamin, his wife, his kids, his life, anything. I fucking challenge you. That doesn't mean if you searched for it, you wouldn't find a clip or two of me discussing the idea that the earth is flat and saying, "You know, I don't quite agree with Owen's opinion on that."

Absolutely we can have disagreements, but I've never shit on the guy, and I've never said anything about him being canceled. And then he flat out accused me of being responsible for Child Protective Services showing up at his house and questioning him about the welfare of his children. He traced it back to a comment made on my show. I had to go back and find out what this was all about, because I never said a bad word about him. I never mentioned his kids or anything, except when I was saying that he seems like a really good dad, and he's got a beautiful wife and a beautiful family.

I absolutely said nothing negative, and then I'm watching him on his podcast saying, "And this motherfucking Anthony Cumia, what's his name...?" Pretending that he didn't know who I was. It's one of those trademark things that radio people do. "…Because of Cumia, Child Protective Services came to my house." And I'm listening to this like, "What the fuck is this all about? Where is he getting this from?" I traced it back to one of my shows where Dave Landau was still the cohost, and we had another comic named Dave Juskow on the show as a guest. We were talking about the flat-Earth concept and flat Earthers, and the fact that Owen had adopted the belief that the earth is indeed flat or at least not spherical. So, as I'm talking about it, Dave Juskow goes, "Wow, maybe Child Protective Services should go check on his kids." After he says that, I immediately go, "Oh, no, no, no, he's a great guy. He's a good dad, great family." I never said anything bad about the guy. It's all on tape. And then Owen fucking shits on me for getting Child Protective Services sent to his house.

And his "Bears," ugh. I'm sorry, but anyone who has a nickname for their little community of podcast listeners is the height of fucking cringe. To no one's surprise, Opie did this for a while with his "Pod Squad." Ugh. "Ah yeah, man, just chatting with the Pod Squad," he'd say. Now it's Owen and his Bears: "Oh, Bear this and Bear that just texted me." But hey, it is what it is.

Anyway, he was ripping me apart for this whole CPS thing. And then he started getting on Gavin McInnes and about the prank Gavin did about an FBI raid of his studio before he left for vacation. I didn't even comment on that prank. A lot of people were like, "Anthony, what happened?" I said, "Let me text him. I'll find out." And I never said or posted another thing about it. That was it. I wasn't going to blow up his spot. It was Gavin's bit; let him do whatever he wants to do with it. And Owen got on a show and just started ripping Gavin apart for a prank that amounted to nothing. Whether you liked it or hated it or didn't think twice about it, there's no reason to get unbelievably angry about it.

Owen, Stuttering John, and Opie are very similar in some ways. Let's review: In my opinion, Stuttering John is incredibly stupid and mentally ill. In my opinion, Opie too is incredibly stupid and mentally ill. And in my opinion, however, Owen is very smart and mentally ill. I will never go off on him as being too stupid to know what he's doing. It's not going to happen. I think he knows everything that he's doing. So, why would Owen light up Gavin like that and criticize Gavin about something that is meaningless, when he could have just said, "Yeah the bit sucked," and left it at that? He tried to make it into some grifter money-grab thing, like Gavin was just doing it for the money. Which is fucking ridiculous. I remember that on the *O&A* show years ago when we would be going on vacation, at the very end of the show we would say something like, "Uh-oh, but I got…" And then *click* and the mic would go off, and the audience would be going, "What was that? What happened?" It's a thing.

But Owen just lost his mind over Gavin's raid prank. Like, he took it as a personal insult and just started shitting all over Gavin, even though apparently, they were friends at the time. Owen then posted a text conversation between himself and Gavin about this and made a whole big thing about "spilling the beans." In the text exchange, Owen wrote, "Are you going to reveal it's a prank? Because I have friends writing blogs about it." Gavin responded, "Never," to which Owen replied, "So you're just going to pretend the FBI raided your studio. Tons of people are texting me freaking out." Gavin wrote back, "I never said they did"— with "they" meaning the FBI and "did" meaning raided his studio.

It's one of those bits. He never actually said the FBI raided his studio. He just left the show's ending ambiguous before he went on vacation. Again, it is what it is. There was no reason for Owen to get that personally invested and offended by this, and then post the whole text exchange about it. He took to Twitter and did this whole post about "spilling the beans": "You really want to run cover for this scam. Everyone takes screenshots of texts like this because believe me, it'll age like mold. A bit has a punch line that arrives, a scam is a lie that's never revealed. Here's the receipts."

Saying that a comedy bit has a punch line with an ending and a scam apparently doesn't suggest that Owen is into making up his own rules in life. That shit may work for your Bears, Owen, but it doesn't hold water for the rest of civilization. You're insane, Owen, and a douchebag. We have receipts.

In the summer of 2023, I was supposed to do a show with Dave Weiss, a.k.a. "Flat Earth" Dave, and Owen, and they were going to debate me on flat Earth. I know. It's really retarded. Then they claimed that I backed out at the last minute, when the truth is that we had asked them if they could do it on a specific date a month prior to doing the actual show, and no one ever got back to us. So, we never booked it. But I told them I'm ready at any time to debate them. I'd do it right now if they wanted to, but now Owen is like, "Nope. I have things to do. Don't you know I run a farm?" Yeah, I know. Anyone who's watched more than two seconds of his show knows that.

You milk goats, Owen? Great, marvelous. You're the most wonderful man on the face of the earth. Everyone else pales in comparison and is an idiot. They're sinners. Whoever isn't you is addicted to porn and alcohol and women and all that stuff. So sad—earthly possessions, materialism, sodomy, all that. No. Owen is the most fucking holy roller of all people placed on here on Earth to judge everyone else. Ugh, enough of fucking Owen Benjamin. Oh my God, when anybody tries to say anything about his ideology, he just has to come up with some personal insults, has to prove that the person is unworthy of living in the world that Owen Benjamin lives in, because Owen's life is so awesome. Yeah, his life is so awesome that he had to move out to the middle of the fucking sticks with his wife and to have a passel of kids. So, now his hands smell like goat tits every fucking day. Does your wife like that, Owen? When you're diddling her with a goat-stink finger?

Yeah, you're just a big common man, right? The earth is flat because no one has proved to you that it's round. Got it. No one went to the moon either, because no one has proved it to you? No one has taken you in a little spaceship to show you the lunar module landing platform on the moon, so I guess that didn't happen either. Until Owen Benjamin says something has happened, it just didn't happen. Flat Earth Dave and Flat Earth Owen and all the other flat Earthers are religious mental patients, because every type of science suggests that planet Earth is a sphere, and explains how it was made and formed, and how it ended up spinning around a giant sun, and how the sun works. Science flies in the face of their faith, which is all they fucking have in the world—their faith in God and Jesus and what have you.

So, in order to keep living and not feel like they should throw themselves off a building, they believe that the earth is five thousand years old and flat, and that God put a roof on it—a.k.a. the firmament. God, how fucking ridiculous does it sound? I think Owen tried to explain the concept scientifically and then threw the religious thing in there. So, God made a big dome out of Plexiglas or whatever the firmament is made of, and there's nothing else like it anywhere. Sure, sure. God made that, and the sun is only five thousand miles up and so is the moon. And everything revolves around Earth, because the planet is filled with humans, and God supposedly made humans in his likeness—again it always goes back to their fucking religious bullshit. And then they just deny the science; they deny your scientific reasoning and figure out why impossible things are actually possible. A flat Earth is impossible. Nothing in our dimension would create a flat Earth with a see-through dome over it. It makes no sense.

And the Lord said, "Let there be a dome." That's how they explain it—God created the dome the same way he created light and everything else. They also believe it's illegal to go to Antarctica, because of the Antarctic Treaty of 1959. Which shows they don't even know how to read, because the Antarctic Treaty specifically says, "Antarctica shall be used for peaceful purposes only." So, it's obviously not illegal to go there if you can use it, and people go there all the fucking time.

Flat Earthers also think Antarctica is one big fucking ice wall that's the edge of the earth, so you can't actually go there and be in Antarctica. We have proof that there are ships that go there and cruises that take people to look at the ice and whatever the hell else is down there. "But planes can't fly to Antarctica" you might hear. Yes, they can. Planes can fly and have flown to Antarctica. Also, flat Earthers like to spew the idea that the perimeter of Antarctica is longer than the equator, which is ridiculous. You mean to tell me that the equator, the line around the center of the spherical planet, is shorter than a circle drawn around Antarctica on a globe? Well, how would they even know, since no one is allowed to go there? It's total bullshit.

Blows their whole fucking argument right out of the water. You're three thousand miles on the start line between day and night. Every single minute of the day. Right now, there's a line between the light and the dark from the north axis. Whatever our situation is, seasonally, but it's a straight line down the earth that circles round every day, two of them. That's impossible from a light source that is three thousand miles up and shining down on a flat, straight line. But people believe it, and they fucking believe the earth is flat. The fucking dunces. They're religious fanatics and impressionable idiots. And Owen Benjamin is extra special, the pride of flat Earth. He's the most noble human to have ever lived, milking goats like a biblical shepherd, with his waxy, greasy, goat-tit-milk-smelling hands. Do you tussle your kids' hair with your goat-tit-milk hands, Owen? God knows what the house smells like with animals running all over the place—pigs, chickens, roosters. Their shit stinks.

You should still have your hands on Christina Ricci's tits, Owen. Those are some nice tits. But now you're just groping at goat tits. When you were engaged to Christina Ricci, you had her two beautiful tits, which I bet smell like bubble gum and homework. But "Oh no, give me a goat. I'd rather have a goat." A stinky fucking goat that pisses on everything and shits pellets all over the house. God, he's lost his mind. The Joe Rogan drug story made him lose his mind. Everything makes Owen lose his mind. Now he thinks the earth is flat. We've never had technology or anything. Apparently, everything is fake except God and goats. Well, Owen, anytime you want to debate, you know where to find me. I'm still here. And to be crystal clear, no one canceled on you at the last minute. There was never a verification, and if one was sent out, we did not receive it, goat boy.

Another thing is that Owen has called me a drunk and a dude who likes porno. You know, the usual great things in life. Yeah, I like to drink. Yeah, I've perused porn. I've looked at naked women. I like the female form; it's pleasant to look at. Plus, would you actually trust a man who doesn't look at porn? No. The answer is no.

But according to Owen, everyone should be some upstanding religious zealot like he is. And drinking and things like that are against the rules of whatever deity he prays to. I don't even know what religion he is exactly. He's just some kind of Christian who thinks everything he does is amazing. A man of the earth, the soil—you know, "The meek shall inherit the earth." And you want to do that? Fine. But don't judge the rest of us. He and everyone else like him are judgmental motherfuckers who feel they have a duty to dress people down and talk about their amazing life.

I can't imagine why anyone would be a religious zealot. But there certainly are religious zealots who act in a very pushy, snobby way, and a lot of them can't fit into society. Owen lives in the middle of fucking nowhere. Yeah, he used to be a stand-up and he drank, but he couldn't take it. He couldn't handle his drinking. I mean, if people can't handle their drinking and they get help and stop, that's great. I'm not going to sit here and bash a guy for getting out of Hollywood, stopping his drinking, and finding some higher power to guide his life. But it's the side effects of all that—the pompous, pretentious shit—that I absolutely will shit on. Yes, I drink, and yes, I look at naked ladies. What are you, Owen, a fucking Sunday school teacher?

Give my regards to the goats.

TRUMPITY
TRUMP TRUMP
● ● ● ● ● ●

WHEN DONALD TRUMP ANNOUNCED HE was running for president in the summer of 2015, I thought we might finally be seeing the light at the end of the tunnel. As you know, I had already been canceled at that point. I had been fired from SiriusXM, and I started up my own video podcast network, Compound Media. Even back then, the cancel-culture phenomenon was really starting to take hold. There were a lot of people who you couldn't goof on and make jokes about, and a lot of people were getting canceled. And when Trump announced that he would be running, I thought, "Oh, this is good. This guy getting into the White House might actually signal that there's a change for the better going on, and maybe we'll be able to start at least handling comedy the way we used to." Where if it's funny, it's funny, and you don't have to care if someone's offended by it.

So, I was very excited when he announced his candidacy in June of 2015. Also, it was the greatest thing for any broadcaster. Trump was pretty much just known for *The Apprentice*, for being very outspoken, and for being a womanizer. And his sense of humor was always a little dark and even dirty, for lack of another word. He had been a guest on the *O&A* show a couple of times and was very friendly with us. And then at one point he called us garbage or trash or scum, and then he was friendly again. So, Donald Trump clearly knew show business, and he was good for show business.

Every show got in on the act of either supporting him or making fun of him, and it was great for the entertainment business. But I was also thinking, "Please, God, make this work for people that are just trying to do comedy." Coming off the heels of Barack Obama, I thought this country really needed to have this guy get into office and concentrate more on America and not so much on opinions and people's emotions. And let's get back to the facts. America first, and true freedom of speech—the right to make jokes about something even if it offends people. So, I was very excited. And as the campaign went on, over the course of the next year, it went from just kind of a joke to, "Holy shit. This guy could win this."

I had faith, and I talked to a lot of people about it too. A lot of comics told me that when they were out on the road all over the country, they'd consider the people in their audiences, the signs on people's lawns and in businesses, and whatnot as an indicator of which way the wind was blowing. And they said the support for Trump was unlike anything they had ever seen. So, a lot of the people that were on the show plus other comics and I were very hopeful that Trump could pull out a victory. And again, not just for the country's sake—having a president who thought that America should come first—but for selfish reasons related to being in broadcasting. I thought, "This is going to be the greatest four fucking years of our lives in broadcasting."

We did a live show on Election Night in 2016 and continued it until the outcome was settled. We had a bunch of guests on the show; the great Nick Di Paolo was on, as well as Gavin McInnes, and a lot of comics would call in to the studio on the phones and on Zoom, and it was an amazing night. I will always remember that as being one of the most fun, interesting, insane shows we ever did on Compound Media. Because here's Donald Trump winning the presidency, and we're going through it in real time, minute by minute; we're checking results, and they were just showing that, oh my God, Trump looks like he's going to win this thing. And on the other side of it is also Hillary Clinton losing it. And we got to watch video clips from the Javits Center in New York, which was supposed to be victory central for Hillary. Having the likes of all those comics and friends and people from other shows on Compound Media being involved in this, and watching these liberals just crying their eyes out, was absolutely fantastic.

So, Trump won the election, and I was feeling pretty good that it might be the turning point. That it might be where everyone—including myself, who had been canceled because of political correctness bullshit, by people being offended by talk about race and sexuality and calling us misogynistic—got to start a new chapter. And in hindsight, I guess I was a bit naive. Things only got worse. The powers that be on the liberal side made it even worse, especially the left-wing media. I didn't understand at the time that the media and Hollywood and Madison Avenue and everything else that pumps imagery and sounds into our eyes and ears were completely against what Trump was doing, how he was trying to turn things around.

I thought things like diversity hires maybe not being based on merit would get turned around for the better, but they only got worse. Again, it kind of made for good show fodder. If you profess to be a comic or an entertainer in any form, you don't want to sit there and agree with the establishment, which is the government and the media and whoever's putting their ideology in front of the people. It's one of the worst things you can do, going along with the establishment. So, it worked well for me as an entertainer—but only because at that point, I had already started my own thing with Compound Media. If I had still been working for Sirius or another radio company, or I was doing a podcast for another company's platform, I'd have been fired ten more times. There was no way that I'd have kept that job, because I wanted to speak my mind. And the thought that maybe Trump being president might have helped people speak their minds without fear of getting fired or canceled was, as I said, kind of naive on my part.

When Trump won on election night, we just looked at the screen dumbfounded—which was kind of the way Trump himself looked when he came out to give his victory speech, saying he was going to do what he could for this country. He was scared shitless, I think. I don't think he believed he'd win. And when the reality of that moment hit him, he looked like, "Oh, shit. I'm the president of the United States." So, that was fun to watch. I think it took him quite a while to become acclimated. A career politician has already been through it by the time they become president, albeit on a smaller scale. They've already been a senator, a member of Congress, a governor, whatever—they've already been in the machine. So, I don't think it's as shocking and as difficult for them to reach the pinnacle of being president as it is for someone with no political experience.

For someone like Trump, I mean, think about it. He was in way over his head when he started. With a lot of the mistakes he made that people point out, particularly some of his early appointments, you have to kind of take into consideration that he was a fish out of water. He wasn't part of the swamp. He had these grandiose ideas that he wanted to do from day one, and I think he got frustrated when he realized they just couldn't be done. Even if you're the president, you can't just get things done immediately. There are so many roadblocks and speed bumps and people with agendas in the way, people who don't want you to accomplish what you want to accomplish, even if it is for the better of the country.

So, I think while Trump tried to figure that out, those of us who supported him kind of wasted time. I think there were a lot of things that could have been done while he had the House, the Senate, and the presidency during the first two years of his term. And I think he had a tough time just getting started. While all of this was good for those of us in broadcasting and comedy, because it made for great subject matter, it seems like the fight against him started day one, with the liberals, the Democrats, and the media just going after him and doubling down on a lot of the shit that made open, honest, and free speech easier.

Coming out of the Obama years, we as a country had just been kicked around like we were kind of a joke. We didn't have the power. The United States needs a powerful leader that isn't going to bow to other leaders. Is it good for a leader to stand in line? A leader needs to be powerful and outspoken first and foremost, not likable. I don't know where the idea came from that a president needs to be likable to be effective. A lot of foreign leaders couldn't stand Donald Trump, which I loved—and it wasn't because he was a bad leader. It's because he was a good leader. And he wanted what was best for America, which wasn't what they wanted. They could push around Obama; to an extent, they were able to push around George W. Bush. Those two had been in politics for so long that they owed people favors, and when those people call in a favor, you can't just say, "Go fuck yourself." Trump could say, "Go fuck yourself," and he did. And I think having that powerful a leader thinking outside the box right out of the gate was a good thing. Trump was like, "Hey, North Korea is acting up. I'm going to go over there and talk to this guy eye to eye. We're going to step over the thirty-eighth parallel, and I'm going to talk to this guy and say, 'Look, we don't need you launching missiles and rockets over Japan, but we're not going to pay you off either, like all these previous administrations did.'"

So, Trump being a strong leader was paramount in his ability to treat China as an enemy. He didn't treat them as an ally. He treated them as what they were and are: competition, a threat. Not buddies. You know, obviously you have to deal with these people and have some dialogue. But what we're seeing now, as far as America's attitude toward China goes, is disgraceful. There's no power there. And when you look at the American government, and you look at a president like Biden, and you know damn well they have shit against them, because Biden is not doing what he needs to do to put America first on the world stage against governments like China and Russia and Ukraine. Trump didn't owe anyone on the political front. So he was able to say, "Go fuck yourself; we're taxing you." Again, him not being a lifelong politician was paramount, I think, to how well the country ran for Trump's first three and a half years as president, before the Chinese decided to pour a plague onto the globe.

For those three and a half years, you could talk to anybody except the most mentally ill liberals, and you would get an honest answer. Plus, wow, I was making money. My company was doing well. Unemployment was down and prices were low, including gas prices. All of these great things were happening that no one wants to talk about now, and that the Biden administration is trying to take credit for, even though Americans and the economy are nowhere near as well off now as under Trump. So yeah, I thought he made a damn good president.

I'm often asked if I think the 2020 election was rigged. Well, how do you define "rigged"? There are plenty of people who honestly believe it was, and maybe it was. I don't know; who the fuck am I? I've been lied to by this government for my entire life. I just woke up to that truth recently, but in hindsight, I realize that these folks have been lying to all of us forever through the use of the propaganda wing, which is the media and Hollywood and Madison Avenue. Those three channels influence the entire country.

So, were the ballots and voting machines tampered with? Look, I'm not going to say no, but I don't think I can honestly say yes either, because I don't know. I don't believe they would ever let you know. But there is something I definitely know: the media tampered with the American people's minds in order to have them vote a certain way. When we think about mind control, we think there's some kind of machine or energy blast, like that old cartoon of Elmer Fudd shooting lightning bolts from his fingers into Bugs Bunny's eyes. Well, there might not be lightning bolts, but there is a form of mind control, and it's the media pounding us over the head constantly with an agenda and an ideology that they present as the right thing: "Here's the right way to think, and here's the wrong way to think." They want us to believe this. So, they shit all over Trump for his entire presidency, and now they've propped up Joe Biden. They won't say anything bad about him, even as we watch him deteriorate from some form of dementia.

The guy's been a liar his entire life. He's plagiarized things, and he's taken credit for things that never happened. And the media have never called him out on it. They didn't even bring up his degenerate son Hunter during the election, while they constantly lambasted Don Jr. and Trump's other kids and called them criminals. And the whole Russian-collusion claim was a lie. We knew that.

And evidence proves that Joe Biden was involved in a quid pro quo with Ukraine. We saw it with our own eyes, and the media told us we didn't. So yeah, the media certainly tampered with people's minds to influence the election.

If you ask me, they had a much bigger influence on "rigging" the election than any number of phony ballots, or dead people voting, or messing with the voting machines. That's the power of the media. So, do I think the election was rigged? Yes, I think it was rigged by the liberal media controlling the agenda and the ideology of the American people to make them vote the way they wanted them to vote. And I think that's easier to do than messing with ballots or voting machines.

Look, I still love Trump. As a selfish entertainer myself, I think first and foremost that he's hilarious. As a leader, he already proved in those three and a half years before COVID that he is able to run a country with that "America first" philosophy that leads to prosperity. Now we're coming up on the 2024 presidential election, and I don't know if I'm being influenced by the media now that I'm aware of it. I hope not. But I don't think any of us can truly say that we're not influenced by such a powerful force. So, in that respect, I see more flaws in Trump than I used to. Does that mean he's more flawed now than he used to be? Again, I don't know. Maybe I'm seeing what the media is putting out there and it's affecting me.

I think Donald Trump is using what worked in 2016, but it's not working quite as well this time around. When he ran in 2016, there were seventeen other Republican candidates, and he blew them out of the water by being smart and funny, giving some of them nicknames, calling them out for what they are, or more importantly, aren't. You know, "Low Energy" Jeb Bush was a great one. So was "Little" Marco Rubio.

All those names were so good, and the media knows they worked. So, when Trump uses these tactics now, the media needs to make it seem bad to the American people, so they won't work again. So now I look at the name-calling and go, "Mmm, maybe Trump shouldn't be doing this. Maybe he shouldn't be calling Ron DeSantis sanctimonious and goofing on him just to get a head start on bashing him in case DeSantis gets the nomination." Now, I think DeSantis is well-received by the American people. I think what he did in Florida over the course of the pandemic was amazing. A lot of people moved to Florida from a lot of the shit cities that had the lockdowns and the mask and vaccine mandates. So, for Trump to start shitting on DeSantis, I see that as a bad move on his part. I don't know how Trump is supposed to handle it, though. If DeSantis becomes a real threat for Trump, they're going to have to somehow go after each other.

I don't think the campaign tactics need to be on such a personal level. I think Trump can run on his record of three and a half prosperous years as president. DeSantis can run on his record of what he's done in Florida, and how he's not one of these establishment guys. They don't need to shit all over each other so that when a candidate finally does get the nod, the other one has to turn around and go, "Well, I said all those things, but it was in the heat of the campaign. We love this guy, and you need to vote for him." It comes off as a little hypocritical and phony.

But I think Trump has a good chance of at least getting the nomination. The thing that I'm most afraid of is that the election will be stolen from him again—not with ballots or faulty voting machines but by the mainstream media going full fucking force against him again and influencing the minds of Americans—who unfortunately, have an average IQ of ninety-eight. And the fact that they have that influence over people who don't know any better is frightening.

Having said all that, I'd 100 percent vote for Trump again if he's the nominee. There's nothing that would get me to vote for a Democratic candidate for president, and I think voting for an independent candidate is a waste of a vote. I think independent candidates take away mostly from the Republican vote, which I don't like seeing. I mean, many of us would love to see a viable third party, but I'll never vote Democrat. And if DeSantis winds up being the nominee, I'll vote for DeSantis. But I do think Trump kind of has to change his tack from his 2016 strategy, like when he told Hillary during a debate that she'd be in jail if he were in charge of the country, or when he called women "fat pigs" and then said really, he was talking about Rosie O'Donnell. All those things were laughing moments, but again, I don't know how well that'd work now.

We're in uncharted territory right now with all of Trump's indictments too. Trump now is kind of proving that if you somehow snuck behind the velvet ropes of the DC version of Studio 54, they will get you, and they will make you pay. He got out and affected the country; he appointed Supreme Court judges. And that goes further than anything a president can do during his tenure in office—appointing those judges who sometimes for decades later are still affecting what goes on in this country. And he did that. So, they couldn't just let him get out and then that was going to be that.

The second he announced his first candidacy in 2015, they went after him. It never stopped, even when he lost in 2020 and voiced his displeasure and his theory and ideology, and especially when he said that the election was not on the up and up. Then they really went after him for what happened in the Capitol on January 6, 2021. There are videos of him speaking about peacefully marching to the Capitol. He got on TV and Twitter a couple hours later and said, "Go home; do not damage anything." I heard about all the things that people said he did that he didn't do. And they have slapped so many indictments on this guy; they've buried him in indictments.

They said in 2015 that they were going to do whatever it took so that Donald Trump would not get elected in 2016. And they thought they had it. They thought Hillary was a shoo-in. Then when Trump won, they did everything in their power to get him out of office—the impeachments, the investigations, the everything. And then when he was no longer in office and questioned the validity of the election, they doubled down on going after him to make sure he doesn't get the fuck back in.

Now, with the 2024 election coming up, they are petrified that this guy might just have a chance of getting in again, and they will never, ever let that happen again. And they've said it. They've stated in public numerous times to numerous people that they will never allow that to happen again. And Donald Trump has said to us for years, "They will not let me get away with this. They most certainly will come after me." And even with that said, people believe that this is a legitimate investigation, and that these are legitimate indictments handed out to the leading candidate for the presidency of the United States. I don't know how half the fucking country is buying into this just sight unseen. They're believing the very people that are going after the guy, so he won't become president again!

You can't trust the indictments. You can't trust anything. And if you don't think that our government is capable of such underhanded shit, like jailing political opponents, then you have just not been paying attention, especially in the past decade. They are capable. They do it. They lie. They're in a partnership with the mainstream mass media that affects people's thought processes and what they believe. People believe in the institution of the news, so they believe what the news tells them, but they don't realize that most of the news is directly connected to the regime in place right now. So, they're not getting accurate information. The only thing anyone knows for sure is that Donald Trump's opponents have said he will never be president again, and that they will do whatever it takes to keep him out of the White House. Those are the only real facts. And you know, perhaps there's a whole lot more bullshit to come.

This is so frustrating, and I'm not saying that as a Trump fanatic. But when you question the indictments on social media, like, "Hey, I've heard things that would lead me to believe that maybe this isn't on the up and up," the argument is always, "Oh, so Trump can do no wrong? You don't think he's a criminal? You don't think this is true?" And that totally misses the point. The point is that Trump is being targeted with criminal charges by his political opponents who will do anything to keep him out of office.

Is Trump guilty of these things? I don't know. I don't think so. I think from what we've seen that there is a valid explanation for his actions, and that he went through the proper channels on January 6, telling people not to do certain things. He was hoping that Mike Pence wouldn't sign off on the election, but he didn't threaten Mike Pence or try to pay him off. He just told Pence, his vice president at the time, "Hey, don't sign off on this fucking thing."

No gun to the head or threats of retribution. And as for asking a group of people to go to the Capitol and show their support for him and show their displeasure with the process, Trump was allowed to do that. Americans are allowed to question an election. There is no law that dictates you cannot question the results of an election, and that questioning firmly falls under the protection of the First Amendment.

After Trump told people to go down there peacefully, the march grew into something that was not peaceful. Who started that? It's questionable. Was it Antifa? Was it the Feds? I haven't seen enough evidence in any direction to tell me who the fuck started this thing. I've seen some shady shit, and I'm not talking far-fetched conspiratorial stuff. I'm talking about people being antagonizing and encouraging other people to go into the Capitol and perhaps do some damage to the windows and doors and whatnot. But that was never investigated, because why look into something when you have the perfect scapegoat? "No, don't investigate, because we have a story here. Donald Trump told people to break into the Capitol and threaten to stop a proceeding that would verify the presidential election results." And it's just not what happened.

But that's what they said happened. Everything that Trump said that day was, "Go down and protest." Yeah, fine, protest. Voice your opinion; show in numbers your support for democracy and the democratic process of this country. You can see and listen to everything he said that day that's been recorded. You can listen to what other people have said and lied about, or you can watch with your own eyes and hear with your own ears what happened. But the people in the media don't want you to do that. They want to squash the general public's ability to find out what actually happened, because they need you to follow their agenda.

So, we got past that whole thing, and now, since Biden has been in there and Trump is running for office again, they have piled more shit on top of this guy. Yeah, Trump questioned the election and said it was bullshit. We saw stuff like the suspicious boxes and the vote counts that shot up overnight—they just went *bam*, straight up. That's questionable. That's something that needed to be looked at. Why did that happen? And did the journalists do any of the actual work that you're supposed to do to investigate any voting discrepancies? Did they actually look into it? We've heard over the years, "Oh, that was debunked." That's another lie. Nothing was ever debunked. They never investigated it. Whenever a case about investigating the 2020 election was brought to a judge, it was thrown out before any investigating could happen. The judge would say, basically, "No, we won't even look at it. There's no validity to this whatsoever, so we're not going to even investigate it." That's not debunking a claim; that's called turning your head the other way instead of looking into it.

So, whenever people go, "Oh, it's a lie about the 2020 election being rigged," how do they know? How can something that was never investigated be a lie? And it's a pretty important fucking thing, since a man could spend his life in prison over it. Yeah, I think it's vital. And this might be the one good thing that comes out of all these legal cases involving Donald Trump: whether the 2020 election was rigged or not is part of discovery. The lawyers can't possibly accuse Trump of committing crimes that depend on the fact that the election wasn't rigged. So now they have to look into that aspect of it. So that'll be interesting, really being able to delve into the election to see if it was indeed fucked up.

I still believe that Trump never did any of the things that he's being accused of and tried for. I'm absolutely disgusted by it all, because we're kind of powerless. Donald Trump was packing arenas. The passion was there for him, and I think it's still there. But the left have this fantasy that if Donald Trump was arrested, that America would go nuts, his supporters would go crazy. There'd be riots. You'd hold back your tax money. You'd take the day and not do anything, so you could see society break down, and that didn't happen. It would have been nice to see some support like that.

And I'll tell you why I believe people aren't showing more public support for Trump in the face of these accusations. People are scared shitless of doing anything that rubs the establishment the wrong way, and that includes the media, the liberal power base, and the Biden administration. They're afraid of going to prison. It's more Stalin than Stalin: jailing, threatening, and intimidating your political opponents. It's Soviet-era tactics that we never would have imagined we could possibly see here in this country, and it isn't even some covert action. This is all being dangled in our faces in real time, and the people in the establishment are doing victory laps.

Biden is fucking gloating that he has tied his political opponent up in a bullshit judicial show—his opponent who's beating him in the polls. And we're all supposed to just sit back and watch people go, "Ha ha, that's awesome." Like we have to be on one side or the other. Democrats will look at this and go, "Yeah, Joe Biden, you go get him," without even thinking that regardless of which side you're on, our country has been put in a really, really terrible position.

In the video of Joe Biden sipping coffee after the indictments were announced, he says, "I like my coffee dark." What is that? It's like Stalin after locking up his political opponents, gloating about it and intimidating other people. The coffee video is an intimidation tactic: "Oh really? You support Trump? Well, look what we just did to him. You want to be next?" It reminds me of the scene in the movie *Airplane* where a little boy and little girl are sitting next to each other on the plane, and a stewardess gives the little girl a coffee and asks if she wants cream, and the little girl says, "No, I take it black. Like my men." She's eight. Biden is being as silly as an eight-year-old girl. He's doing a victory lap over his side's intimidation of his number-one political opponent. They are intimidating and mocking Trump and his supporters, and they're gloating about it. This is beyond Soviet tactics.

Before 9/11, I truly never thought I would see days like this. In news footage from Jerusalem or Tel Aviv, you'd see soldiers standing at the train stations and airports and entertainment venues. And I'd look at that and think how lucky we are to live in a place where we don't need armed soldiers just standing around locations that we take for granted are safe just because we're America.

We Americans kind of have a common code of ethics and morality, in that we wouldn't want to just go into a bus station and blow up a bunch of people. But it's normal everyday life in Tel Aviv and Jerusalem and a lot of other places in the Middle East, and having to actually live under those circumstances is kind of fucked up. Then 9/11 happened, and it was the first time I remember seeing soldiers with their rifles at public places where you never would have seen them before. And when I was over the initial "Oh, cool. It's an army man," it hit me: "Oh, fuck. That's it. Now we're this, and we have to have this going on." It was so unimaginable, until it wasn't. And it's the same thing with these Soviet tactics going on in America today: jailing and intimidating political opponents, squashing free speech and freedom of expression, and totally taking away people's ability to defend themselves and their families the way they deem fit. I just never thought that was coming.

But just like with the soldiers at the airport, it happened. And it's just as obvious, by the way, the political oppression and subversion happening right now. These motherfuckers have their boot on your neck and are not allowing you to voice your opinions. Not allowing you to choose a leader that you want to vote for. The motherfuckers are throwing your leader in fucking jail so you can't vote for him. It's just as obvious as soldiers at the airport. Let's be real. How much more benefit of the doubt are you going to give these motherfuckers? Even when that fucking boot is firmly on your throat, you probably will still go, "Well, maybe he needed to rest his foot somewhere, and my throat was just the closest thing to it." Wake up. Fight back. Stop the bullshit and open your eyes.

CANCEL THIS CANCEL CULTURE BULLSHIT! ENOUGH ALREADY!

● ● ● ● ● ● ●

OBVIOUSLY THE FIRST THING THAT stands out about the Black Lives Matter movement that started with George Floyd is the hypocrisy of it all. It became a movement not so much about black lives mattering; the thing that mattered was who was perpetrating the crimes against black people. So obviously, you know, if a white person has a problem with a black person and something happens—whether it's a fight or just a discussion or murder—it's going to be a big story. The media will pick up on it. They'll talk about the racism in this country, and how horrible white people are.

But when you see a lot of instances that are the other way around—where black people are perpetrating crimes and violence against white people—the media just will not acknowledge it. There are many of these cases that happen every day in every city in this country, but you just don't hear about them for a plethora of reasons. But when an incident like the one with George Floyd occurs—and it always happens every few years; we have the Trayvon Martin thing, and then the George Floyd thing—the media really pile on and make white people seem like a horrible, oppressive, murderous group that is the cause of every problem in the black community.

Here's what I believe about George Floyd. From everything I've read, he died of a drug overdose in the custody of police officers who were trying to take him in. He was fighting; he had enough drugs in his system that would be fatal to anybody. And then when he did die, they needed someone to blame it on, and of course, the evil white police officers were a great scapegoat. This led to the riots, and then Black Lives Matter popped up, which is ridiculous in and of itself. I mean, I love an organization whose name is Black Lives Matter, and if you say that all lives matter, the supporters get pissed and call you a racist. So right from the start, it was bullshit. The only problem is, you're not even allowed to address the bullshit or talk about it in any way, shape, or form.

Now I, of course, do a comedy-based show where I get into politics and pop culture and whatever else is in the news that day, but for the most part, I like to keep it light, making jokes about things that you're not "allowed" to joke about, like the ridiculousness that is Black Lives Matter. Pointing out the hypocrisy of it. You watch shows like *Saturday Night Live* and all the late-night talk shows, and they don't talk about it. Why? Because it's not a popular topic. It's not a topic that is being discussed by everybody. Well, that's not true, of course it is. You're just not allowed to discuss it.

You hear all the time from supposed community leaders and whoever else that we need to have an open and honest discussion about race in this country. But the second you *are* open and honest about it, you are called a racist. Then they'll demand that you apologize, so they can then throw you out of your job and society and whatever else they can throw you out of. We need the opportunity to honestly discuss racial matters in this country, but we're not allowed to.

Again, the media are one of the main culprits in this whole thing. They write the narrative, telling everybody what they can and can't talk about, and they will absolutely crucify people who are open and honest in a discussion or a debate. And then they cancel those people. That's what cancel culture is. Cancel culture is based on, "We don't like what you've said. It doesn't suit our agenda." There are protected communities in America that are never to be discussed by people not in that community. And anyone thinking that that's a good thing is a fucking idiot. I think if any problem is ever going to be solved in this country, it'll happen by honestly talking about it and not threatening people with losing every bit of their livelihood and lives if they do even discuss it at all.

I get on the air and talk about Black Lives Matter all the time, but I can only do that because I have my own company. I literally had to make a broadcast company just so I could talk about shit that I was not allowed to talk about on anyone else's platform. How insane is that? I remember going from broadcast radio to satellite radio and everyone was like, "Isn't that great? You're going to be able to say so many things and talk about forbidden topics and curse." And at first I thought, "It's okay, because wow, look, I'm finally allowed to say the word 'fuck.'" But for me personally, it was more fun trying to get around how to discuss titillating topics on FM radio than it was to just be able to say "fuck" on satellite radio.

But my real attraction to satellite radio at the time was that I was going to be able to discuss taboo topics. We were going to talk about race and sexuality and all that stuff. Well, I learned quickly enough that you are not allowed to discuss any of these topics on or off the air. If you recall, I got fired for tweeting something that had nothing to do with my employer, SiriusXM satellite radio. I simply voiced my opinion on a topic on a separate media platform and was fired for it. The media labeled what I said a racist diatribe. A diatribe? Not even close. I never even used racial slurs. I only talked about what happened to me, which was being assaulted by an African American woman in Times Square and not fighting back. I left the scene and went back to my apartment and voiced my disgust and my opinion on how and why that jump to violence happened. And then I was summarily fired for doing nothing but being completely honest about what had just happened to me.

How are we, as a society and as individuals, supposed to solve any of these issues if we are not even allowed to talk about them? Like I said, I had to make my own company so that I could talk about the multitude of racial crimes perpetrated against white people by people of color on a daily basis. Why should I have to put myself in the safe little capsule of my own company in order to do this? Shouldn't we be allowed to talk about this? Shouldn't the mainstream media address this? How are things going to get better if we're not even allowed to publicly address the issue?

Callers ask me all the time on my show, "Anthony, where does this go from here? Does it get better? Does it get worse? What's the conversation going to look like in five years or ten years? Is the pendulum going to swing back to the little fragments of normalcy that we can barely remember from the past? What's going to happen?" The truth of the matter is that I've had so many false alarms in believing that things were getting better, or that they were going to get better. It's like you can see a glimpse of the proverbial light at the end of the tunnel, and then you realize it's a train barreling down on you.

I really kept thinking things were going to get better, that they had to, because everything swings back and forth. But when you have a propaganda-driven media, there's no getting the pendulum to swing the other way. It's now their agenda to make sure it doesn't. They realize they can now be one-sided with impunity. I think they used to have to take the other side every so often just so people wouldn't think they were full of shit and pounding a single agenda. Now they don't seem to care. Every single broadcast by the mainstream media is now totally agenda-based, and they don't even have to pretend anymore that they're being unbiased. They just show what they want to show, and they have no qualms about destroying anyone with an opposing viewpoint and just moving along.

So, I think right now we are in such a bad position to solve this issue and to be able to speak openly, honestly, and freely without fear of life-altering repercussions. And I don't see that changing anytime soon, or maybe even ever. But make no mistake about it, freedom of speech as we used to know it is done. And it's probably not coming back. In the environment we live in today, you can lose your livelihood now if you speak freely. And I hate hearing people say, "Well, we have freedom of speech in the sense that the government can't come down on us and curtail our freedom to speak our opinions or practice our religions or anything else covered under the First Amendment."

Well, when you are under the threat of losing your livelihood, that's a pretty big deal. And it doesn't matter that it's not the government threatening you, that it's your employer and your bosses that don't like what you have to say. Well, that's still an absolute infringement on freedom of speech. I don't care that it's not the government doing that—it's a power. Your employer has power over you. That's how most people earn their living.

So, maybe right now you have a roof over your head, you have food, and you can raise your family. But if you express a viewpoint that goes against the liberal media, you could lose all that. And it's fine because it's not the government doing it? No. That is not what the essence of the First Amendment and freedom of speech is. But people absolutely believe it. This is why you have people like Ann Coulter and Gavin McInnes, and a lot of public speakers, such as Alex Stein, who want to go to colleges—the so-called bastions of freedom of speech, openness, and learning—and speak to a group of people who want to hear them, but more times than not, a group of left-wing lunatics on campus will put up a fight so they can't. And the worst part isn't even that they're preventing the speakers from being able to enlighten the audience, which of course is part of it and what they want you to think. Their lunatic narrative is, "Look, we're against this horrible fascist Nazi guy, so we're going to prevent him from speaking." Well, it's easy to say that. What's really happening would be a lot harder to sell to people, which is, "We're preventing you, the students and everyone else on campus, from hearing what that person wants to say."

When you keep someone from speaking at your college because you don't like their opinion, what you're really doing is preventing other students—who have a right to go see the person and absorb what they want to say—from actually hearing them and their viewpoints. And how do you justify that? How do you cheer on people who want to prevent other people from hearing dissenting opinions and differing opinions?

The projection of the left wing in this country is utterly astounding. Leftists are everything they accuse the right wing of being. That's the kind of dystopian *1984* vibe that we have in this day and age. When you call yourself an anti-fascist, you are actually the fascist, but because you call yourself an anti-fascist, the media can then present you as that. And then they'll call the people who are actually *for* the freedoms of Americans—like Ron DeSantis down in Florida—fascists. Why? Because he lets the people in his state decide what they want to do with their lives? How do you call that fascism?

It's the exact same thing politicians do with legislative bills. They give these bills names that have nothing to do with the actual bill, and if you are against the bill, you seem like an asshole. Like maybe you're against the "Feed the Hungry" bill, which is actually a climate change thing, and it never has anything to do with the actual name of the bill, but then when the elections roll around, your opponents can go, "Hey, he didn't sign the Feed the Hungry bill. He doesn't care about starving Americans."

A prime example was the Inflation Reduction Act, which Biden signed into law in August 2022. If you believe the title, it was designed to fight inflation, but to no one's surprise, it actually had nothing to do with inflation. It was like a green New Deal targeting climate change, another boondoggle with money going to insane programs. And if you didn't vote for it, they could then present you as being against cutting inflation: "Well, my fellow citizens, my opponent didn't vote for the Inflation Reduction Act. He is clearly pro-inflation." Bullshit.

Well, how do you let people know that it's bullshit, and that their government is lying to them? Well, you do it on political shows, talk shows, and podcasts. That's what I like doing on my show. But unless you're the likes of Joe Rogan, you're rarely going to be able to reach as many people as mainstream media does. So, you constantly find yourself shoveling shit against the tide, even though you know you're right, and you know you're being lied to, and it's frustrating that so many people don't see it. One of the things I write the most at the end of some of my controversial tweets is, "Open your fucking eyes because the truth, it's right in front of you." The idea that people can't see it when it's right in front of them is extremely alarming.

Again, why would you trust the government when it has done nothing to earn your trust? They people in government have done nothing but lie to you. There are many examples out there. You could watch videos of them saying something one day and then the complete opposite thing the next day. And still people will just dig in with their ideological tribe and go, "I'm on this side. I need to stay with my team. So, I'm just going to go down with the ship and lie right along with them." Well, that doesn't make for a good country, and it's certainly not helping make this country what it used to be. In fact, that attitude is entirely responsible for what this country is quickly spiraling into.

Another question I get all the time is, "How does the ordinary citizen deal with this on an everyday basis? Is it basically just keep your mouth shut and don't offend anybody? Go forward and accept what the media is telling you and be PC and follow the line? How does the ordinary citizen possibly go about this and safely navigate these waters?"

Unfortunately, the average American Joe and Jane, who work for a living—you know, trying to earn enough money to keep the house going and put their kids through school and whatever else—are so tied up with just keeping their fucking noses above water that they don't have the time or energy to fight what is keeping them in that shitty situation. So, for the most part, people have to go to work, and when they come home from work, they just want to spend that time away from work having whatever simple pleasures they can and not making too many waves.

The oppression we're facing now is a slow boil. No one is throwing scalding water in your face, but the temperature of the water you're sitting in has been going up and up and up, and you're just sitting there not realizing you're being boiled. I think the expectations that American citizens have are pretty low these days. As long as you're paying most of your bills every month and your son or daughter isn't in jail, you probably consider yourself to be pretty lucky. Because what the left-wing media and the government are telling you about how awesome they are and how they're making your life better is a crock of shit. We can see it with our own eyes. This shit is happening every day right in front of us.

And like I said, as long as you walk out your front door in the morning and someone isn't shooting you and you have a job to go to, you consider yourself lucky. Well, fuck that. It can be so much better. This country can be so much fucking better. But we're being held hostage by special-interest groups—racially focused groups, gender identity groups. They are a small fucking percentage of the population, but they have all this power to ruin your life. So, I think every regular ordinary working American citizen is petrified to even bring up any issues that contradict them.

Over the past several years, I've talked with and interviewed so many people on my show from damn near every profession who are disgusted about the direction this country is going in. Take comedians, for example. I've had plenty of comics on the show who are petrified to touch on what they deem controversial topics. I get that, and when I have someone on as a guest, I don't go off on topics like I would on a solo show.

Look, I'm blessed with the ability to say whatever the fuck I want on my show, but I know that when certain comments come in, I have to hold back. I don't want to put my friends and people who have good careers in a bad position by bringing up a topic that they'll be fucked for just because they were in the same room as me when I talked about it. So, I don't do that. I'm not trying to pull a "gotcha" moment on anybody. But it makes me feel bad that they are actually petrified that at any moment their career could be pulled out from under them for a slip-up—for saying something that's not even bad, just an opinion that isn't what the mainstream media, liberals, and Democrats are saying. Try commenting on race. Go ahead. Be a comic who has a clean act, does the late-night talk-show circuit, and has an opinion on a racial topic that differs from the narrative. Maybe you bring up crime stats that are so fucking out of control that anyone should be talking about it.

Do that and watch your career go down the toilet. And why? Because you had the audacity to bring up a fact? It's such a shame, and I've seen it happen—not just with my own cancellation experience either. It's no wonder that people are looking over their shoulder and are scared shitless about getting canceled, and I fucking feel bad for them. That's a paranoia that you just can't run away from. Plus, being unable to voice your opinion only creates resentment toward the people you're not allowed to talk about. So, when you get canceled or are petrified of being canceled, because a certain group has deemed it impossible for you to comment on them, you're clearly going to resent that group. It's basic human nature. And I couldn't be happier that I'm not beholden to that.

As for an overall message that I'd offer to my fans and members of the general public that have yet to be brainwashed by the lunatic left's propaganda, it's this: If you can figure out a safe topic, go ahead and talk about it. Be especially careful if you want to pursue a career in any aspect of the entertainment business that is open to public scrutiny. In this day and age, unless you're going to do a podcast or other broadcast about the most vanilla, nothing topics, you're at risk of being canceled. And if you are petrified of being canceled, and especially if you have a job you love and a family to support, then please do yourself a favor and stay the fuck away from podcasting or any other kind of broadcasting.

Stay away from social media too. Don't post on Twitter. Don't go to Instagram. Don't do anything, because it can only fuck with your livelihood in ways you don't want to imagine becoming your reality. You are only putting yourself out there to be criticized by people who make it their goal in life to destroy anyone with a differing opinion. And the only thing that can come back to you is trouble and cancellation and a scarlet letter. You'll be accused of racism or misogyny or any other shit you can be pegged with, just because you put your personal opinion out there. There is no fucking upside to posting shit on social media about your feelings on controversial topics, unless you are willing to take the hit.

Many people over the years have experienced a shit-storm for something they said or wrote, whether they did it intentionally or whether they were just being open and honest. Some of them picked themselves up and started their own companies, like myself and Gavin McInnes did. But unless you're completely prepared to get shat on and possibly lose some valuable parts of your life because you are passionate enough to want to speak your mind, just stay away from controversial topics entirely. Because that's the world we live in. In no way, shape, or form is there anything resembling freedom of speech in this county.

Another question I often get is, "How do we win this fight?" And believe me, it is a fight, and it always will be. "Is this fight winnable? Or are we stuck having to conduct ourselves according to the new narrative and conform to what's being thrown at us? Is there anything that we can do about this?" Well, the only good part in this whole situation—and it might seem like a bad part, but it is the only way this can get better—is the fact that they can't stop. The train has already left the station. They have to make things worse and worse, and put more and more infringements on our rights. They will curtail more and more of what we are under God allowed to do, so it will affect more and more people who normally wouldn't become involved.

It has to get to a point where enough people can clearly see what's happening and how they're affected by it. But we're not there yet. I don't think we're even close to getting there. People today are still like, "Hey, look at this guy Anthony Cumia and this guy Gavin McInnes. They are talking about race issues and discrimination and gender. I agree with them, but I don't want to touch that." Okay, I totally get it. You don't want to lose your shit. You have opinions that you'd rather keep quiet. But here's the thing: they won't stop there.

Let's say you just bought an Escalade. You thought, "Hey, I'm doing well. I'm going to treat myself and buy an Escalade. Let me post a picture of me with my brand-new Escalade."

Now, you're thinking it's so innocent, right? But then someone with a certain agenda sees your picture and reposts it on their social media platforms and goes, "Look at this person destroying our environment, using his white privilege to destroy the air we breathe. His carbon footprint must be huge, and we can't allow people like him to get away with this!" And now you're a piece of shit in the eyes of a lot of people who have different beliefs than you.

The leftists will never stop. They will push their agenda further and further down our throats, until so many ordinary citizens get affected by their bullshit that they finally decide to do something about it. For things to possibly turn around, enough people have to say, "Alright you shitbags, fuck this! I've had enough!"

And then we just let the left continue to do what they've been doing, which is eating their own. Like with Don Lemon on CNN—other libs will hear something he said that they disagree with, and they'll accuse him of saying something that offended women. They'll always eat their own because, look, these people are hypocrites. They will always be hypocrites. Someone in their little club will slip up, and the other liberals will kick that person out of their club and destroy him. So, when that has happened enough times, I think it will open the eyes of a lot of people, and then we can start turning this fucking insane tanker ship of political correctness around.

If I had any kind of parting message to leave you with, I would say keep fighting the fight on whatever level you're able to. And look, I understand there are people who don't want to lose everything. I get that no one wants to lose what they work for. But you have to put up some kind of fight. I'm not talking about going on social media and blowing up your fucking career talking about race or trans-gender rights or bathrooms or fucking misogyny or which women shouldn't be having kids or patriotism and stand-ing or kneeling for the National Anthem at sporting games. I'm not even talking about going that far. But at least voice that you're not fucking happy with the way things are going and that you have taken note of people who have lost everything just for voicing their opinion, regardless of what that opinion is.

You don't have to agree or disagree with anyone's opin-ions. But you should agree that people shouldn't be can-celed and lose everything just for voicing their fucking opinion. So yeah, fight as hard as you can without putting your entire livelihood at risk. At least let people know that you don't like the way things are going.

In closing: fuck them!